Hecklers In Your Crowd

Hecklers In Your Crowd

Silencing The Voices That Hold You Back

J. L. Acevedo

To my darling wife Doreen and my two beautiful daughters, Amanda and Sara. You all are my joy and crown. Thanks for the dreams and many laughs. You have made life a great adventure. To my extended family at Lake Washington Fellowship, you are the best congregation a pastor could hope for. Thanks for your priceless encouragement, prayers, and for releasing me so I could write. To the brave few that read the manuscript in its raw state before it was edited. It was a brutal task but you did it anyway. Thanks for your input. I am indebted to you. To the folks who inspired me and challenged me to press on (you know who you are), thanks for believing in me.

Table of Contents

Let the disruption begin!

THAT MAN MUST have thought I was the son of Satan. Although it wasn't my original intention to create mayhem and drive him absolutely insane, in time it certainly became that way. A church choir can be a great, fun experience—unless there's a disruptive person like me in it.

When I was a teenager, my parents started going to a Spanish church in Orlando, Florida. Every Sunday they forced me to go along with them. The whole idea of God was against my nature at the time, but on Sunday mornings Dad would stand at my bedroom door 'playing' Reveille on an imaginary trumpet. As much as I hated the whole scene, I would do as he asked and away we would go.

Soon thereafter I found out there were some cute *senoritas* in that church and I started getting up on my own. Before long I joined the youth choir. Mind you, I was not interested in making a joyful noise unto the Lord. I just wanted to get to know some of those girls in hopes of connecting with one of them.

I was joyfully welcomed with open arms into the rehearsal, but I soon started giving that choir director absolute H-E-DOUBLE HOCKEY STICKS during rehearsals. From the top row of the loft I did everything in my power to disrupt and dismantle whatever that volunteer leader was trying to do. I had become a heckler in his choir (his crowd)!

Week after week it would not take long for that man to become frustrated with my ridiculous antics. His face would go from light tan to cherry red in a hurry. I am sure he had a good heart and prayed for every one of us teens, but I wonder how fervently he asked the Lord above to move my family to another church.

A common phrase in our English language is that hindsight is 20/20. Had he known that God was training me at his expense, that I was a pastor in the making, he may have handled it differently! But there's no way he could have foreseen that.

Maybe as you read these words you find yourself where that choir leader was, with a heckler in your crowd. Your heckler (the person giving you a difficult time) could be someone you work next to, live by, or worship with. Your heckler may even be related to you.

Hecklers have the uncanny ability to throw a bucket of cold water on your fire or break up your daily routine in order to annoy you and get the best of you. You may call a heckler something else: clown, devil incarnate, witch, or maybe even an expletive title that would not be proper for me to write down. But they all refer to the same person you have issues with.

Negative people have a tendency to get on your nerves, don't they? Sometimes they are the reason you want to stop trying. Hecklers can even make you want to give up your plans before you start them. Hecklers are a load on your shoulders, a thorn in your flesh, and a pile of junk in your trunk.

Anyone or anything can become a heckler in your crowd at any given moment. It could be an insensitive neighbor allowing his dog to bark incessantly in the middle of the night, depriving you of much-needed sleep and rest. It could be an unforeseen illness in you or in someone you know and love that brings havoc to your life.

I had the privilege of being a police chaplain for seventeen years. The Lord used that ministry to reach officers and supporting personnel for His kingdom, and I am extremely thankful for that time. My duties included befriending the officers and being on call to assist them whenever they deemed necessary. One time I was called to the scene of an apparent suicide. My job that night was to be present and assist one of the officers informing a loved one of the tragedy that had taken place before that person reached the location where the victim was. The deceased had used a lipstick and written a lot of gibberish on the bathroom mirror and walls. Mental illness had become a heckler—not only in that person's life but also in the lives of those left behind.

One afternoon I was asked by the police department communications center personnel to wait at the hospital for the daughters and wife of a certain businessman in town. He had been playing golf that day but suffered a massive heart attack on the eighteenth hole and died. His loved ones had been called to the hospital but did not yet know exactly what had happened. I met them in the Quiet Room in the hospital and regretfully informed them of his passing. The family was devastated. Death had become a heckler in their crowd.

Anything that disquiets you, anyone who harasses you or brings conflict to your life, could be described as a heckler. Sometimes the threat to your inner harmony comes from an unexpected source. Sadly, though, most of us are not ready to handle whatever negativism a heckler may surprise us with. As a result, we feel the sting of words and actions only after the damage is done in our lives.

I was getting ready to perform a wedding ceremony for two good friends of mine. It was a perfect day for an outside river's edge wedding. While preliminary pictures were being taken of the bride and her maids, I found a nice, quiet place under a tree to refresh my memory of what I was going to be saying during the ceremony. I unbuttoned my suit, opened my Bible, and stood there reading and meditating.

Suddenly I felt as if a bright white angel had momentarily passed before me. I was startled! It happened in an instant. I looked around hoping to catch another glimpse of him, her, or whatever it was but did not see anything. By then it was time to start the ceremony so I closed my Bible, buttoned up my suit, and forgot all about it.

After the wedding, the photographer started taking pictures of the happy couple in the beautiful surroundings while my lovely wife, Doreen, and I found a cozy seat for two under a palm tree to enjoy the celebration. I unbuttoned my suit to relax when she looked at me and asked, "What in the world is that?" She pointed to a generous amount of white bird poop on my shirt and tie. Then it hit me: what I thought was an exciting angelic appearance before the wedding was nothing more than a bird overhead laying some bad lunch on me. It had been hidden from sight while my suit was buttoned.

I went to the bar and dipped a napkin in water to try to clean up the mess. A guy next to me said, "You were tagged by a bird? Nice! That means you are going to have good luck." Really? My mom used to say the same thing to me when I was a kid and I would step on one of my dog's "land mines" in the backyard. I'm still not convinced.

Throughout life, people you think are harmless, good for you, even heaven-sent, will try to make a mess of your life. They are hecklers in your crowd. Hecklers also come in the form of ugly, difficult, hurtful situations. My purpose in writing this book is to help you effectively identify and defeat whatever comes your way. In the pages that follow I am going to identify several potential hecklers and describe how to successfully overcome them.

In my line of work I often encounter heartbroken, defeated people who are being railroaded, gossiped about, or cheated. Sometimes the problem is not an individual but a set of circumstances that is making you miserable. The Lord does not want you to live defeated under those circumstances but be victorious over them.

Keep in mind that misery is not the company God intends for you to keep. Instead God wants you to enjoy the fruit of His Spirit: love, joy, peace, patience, kindness, goodness, faithfulness, gentleness, and self-control (Galatians 5:22-23). I would rather take those over misery any day! The wise man wrote, "Better a dry crust eaten in peace than a house filled with feasting—and conflict" (Proverbs 17:1).

The Lord will give us peace when we trust Him. In Him you can choose to be a victor rather than a victim. Conqueror rather than conquered.

It was a Sunday morning like any other. I was behind the congas playing Latin percussion in the church's band with my thoughts on the sermon I was about to preach. Doreen was in her usual spot in the back of the auditorium, last row, singing and enjoying the worship. Then everything changed.

On Sunday mornings we always have a meet and greet time between music sets. I was hugging some of our people when I looked over and noticed a troubled look in my bride's face.

I had seen that face before when she received an unexpected phone call from her sister, who was calling to inform her that their mom had slipped into a coma after a brain aneurysm and that there was not much hope. My darling was shocked and dismayed. All of us were. Her look was one of contained panic. She was almost dazed as if her very life had been sucked from within her.

Doreen had that same anxious, heartbroken look in her eyes during our meet and greet, so I quickly rushed to her side. She had received a call. Our younger daughter, Sara, in her early twenties at the time, was being rushed to the emergency room. She had been held down and severely beaten by someone who hated her. Our older daughter, Amanda, was already at the hospital with her, along with police officers.

You must understand that Doreen and I love our daughters with all of our hearts. We would do anything for them. We see them as precious gifts God has entrusted into our care, and we take that responsibility seriously. But what was going on was beyond our control. There was absolutely nothing we could do at the moment.

The stress, the bully who had attacked Sara, and the deep hurt in my heart had all become hecklers in my crowd. They threatened to crush my spirit and disrupt my life, and I did not know how to silence them!

In those brief few seconds of conversation, my wife and I rationalized that our hurting daughter was already with her sister and in the care of emergency doctors. There was not much we could do at the moment but pray and wait. A close friend volunteered to go with Doreen, so she encouraged me to stay back and preach, and afterwards to meet her at the emergency room.

Only a handful of friends in our congregation knew what was going on that morning. We did not want to hinder the work the Holy Spirit of God was already doing through the service, so we simply asked those who knew to please pray for our daughter's wellbeing and for the Lord to help me preach His Word.

As Doreen and her friend exited the building, I quickly went to my office, got on my knees, and prayed. I pleaded for God's healing touch on my child. I also asked the Lord to help me gather my thoughts and focus on Him. Preaching is His time, not mine.

I went back to my place in the band, but all I could think about was what my girl was going through. During the last song before the sermon—and in desperation—I silently prayed, "Lord, my mind is on my baby girl. I can't share Your message unless You refocus me to what You want me to say. Please help me stay composed. It's your time, God. I need You; help me overcome."

The last song was over and I stepped up to the lights. I glanced at those key few in the congregation who knew what was happening and were silently praying. I opened my mouth and almost broke down. I paused briefly. Mentally I threw myself unto God to keep me emotionally in check and began speaking. I was able to deliver the whole sermon without a hiccup and the Lord spoke that morning in a great way.

The moment I finished speaking, I left for the hospital and finally saw my daughter in the emergency room. I broke down then. At the time Doreen received the call, all we knew was that our daughter was hurt. At the hospital we came to know the severity of Sara's wounds. Emergency room doctors feared not only a broken nose but also the possibility of a brain hemorrhage, brain damage, and loss of vision. She had received many blows to the face and head without having an ability to defend herself.

Today I am happy to report that the Lord took good care of her. His angels had been standing guard by her side that day. She is fully recovered from her injuries and doing great in life.

Later that day, those who knew what happened asked me, "How were you able to do that? How could you preach under those circumstances? I wouldn't have been able to do what you did."

On my own I was doomed to fail, but somehow, someway, something great happened. The Spirit of the Lord silenced the hecklers trying to hold me back! He gave both my wife and me the faith we needed to believe that He would take care of the situation. He also gave us the wisdom and strength to deal with and overcome that tough time.

In the pages that follow I want to provide you with ideas and examples on how you, too, can silence the disrupting hecklers in your crowd that try to hold you back. Do not let the negative voices that want to see you fail prevail. With God's help you will overcome!

At the end of each chapter is a section called *What's Your Take?* This section has thought-provoking questions that encourage discussions in a small group setting. Enjoy!

PART 1

Ambushed!

1

Who's That Heckler?

*Antagonists are to our emotions what phlebotomists
are to our veins, sucking the life out of us.*

THERE MAY HAVE been twenty-five people at church that Sunday morning. I had not been the pastor there long. Then something unusual happened that taught me to always try to expect the unexpected. While I was in the middle of preaching time, one of the choir members behind me blurted out something, interrupting the message.

I have been in exciting congregations that respond to the preacher. "Aha, go on, you got that right, brother," they will reply to a pastor's statement. That kind of thing tends to rev up the Rev. But the man in the choir that morning was not trying to charge me up—he was trying to shoot me down.

He was shaking me off like a pitcher shakes off his catcher's signals. He had a scowl on his face. His eyebrows were down and his eyes penetrating, like semi-automatic weapons shooting daggers my way. With angry, pungent words he yelled, "You got-ta be kidding me, brother George." It was clear the old white-haired choir member in the loft had issues with the young preacher in the pulpit. I took a quick glance behind me, kept my composure, and preached on as if nothing unusual had happened.

A few moments later there was another rude comment from the disgruntled church member. "You are wrong, pastor! What you're saying ain't right." This time he was even waving his arms in the air as if wanting me to walk off the podium and leave right in the middle of Sunday morning church! I had a heckler in my choir, my crowd!

At this remark I stopped the sermon mid-stream (big mistake), turned around, and started arguing with the man about the Biblical point I was trying to share with the congregation. Every time I get to speak God's Word, I work hard at being as accurate to the Scriptures as possible. Accuracy and relevancy are top priorities. I do not take lightly anyone who questions the integrity of Scripture and its message.

Stop for a moment! Think. How would you have handled that situation if you were in my shoes?

A. Ignored the man
B. Thrown your Bible at him
C. Asked the dude to hang up his choir robe on the way out
D. Argued theology with the parishioner
E. Told him to get a life
F. All of the above

The scene that morning made everyone uncomfortable and embarrassed. It was just random and awkward. When the exchange was over I went on to finish the sermon. The antagonist then (and for the rest of the sermon) turned his chair sideways and faced the wall as if he was on time-out. Can you imagine?

I'll refer to the heckler as Mr. G. This happened many years ago and I'm sure he is dead by now, but when he was alive I felt like his spiritual purpose was to bring me down.

In the weeks and months that followed, Mr. G tried other creative ways to mess me up while I preached. Sometimes he would hide his face behind the oversized 3-fold Sunday program we used in those days. Had he thought of it he might have even worn a paper bag over his head with cutouts for his eyes and a frown drawn on it.

What bothered me most is that Mr. G was one of the people I had ministered to and trusted. I had been to his home and prayed with him and his family during their times of crisis and need. Mr. G had even privately told me how much he cared for me.

Maybe you too have worked on a church staff and faced the wrath of the chosen frozen. However, you do not have to work in church to face hecklers. They tend to appear in any and every field of endeavor. If you deal with people on a regular basis you will face hecklers in your crowd. It's a fact of life.

Double-Barreled Thinking

I want to share two words that can toughen you up for when the going gets tough. Like a double-barreled shotgun that fires and hits multiple places at once, these words pack some divine punch. But before we get to those two words please remember that the same God who calls you keeps you! When you follow Jesus, your decision is backed by His provision.

You may be familiar with Psalm 37:4 (NIV): "Take delight in the Lord, and he will give you the desires of your heart." What a wonderful, powerful verse of promise! But most people don't know the verses before and after that one. I am going to bunch verses three and five together because the thought flows nicely even without verse four being sandwiched between them. "Trust in the LORD and do good. Then you will live safely in the land and prosper... Commit everything you do to the LORD. Trust him, and he will help you" (Psalm 37:3,5 NIV).

Sounds incredibly promising, does it not? I want you to remember two verbs: *trust* and *commit*.

Trust, having faith, is opposite to having doubts. Hecklers often make us doubt ourselves: our calling, our vision, and our decision to do what we can for the Lord. Staying on task, remaining confident, doing what you know you are supposed to do, and being true to who you are as a person are critically important.

Trust requires the certainty that the Lord is with you regardless of what happens. When you trust, you are declaring that your heavenly Father knows your name; your address; your career; your past, present and future; your dreams, goals, associations and interactions; your down times; your good times; your sad times; your stressed-out times; and everything else in between. It just feels good to know that your God is presently at your side at all times.

After His powerful resurrection, "Jesus came and told his disciples, 'I have been given all authority in heaven and on earth. Therefore, go and make disciples of all the nations, baptizing them in the name of the Father and the Son and the Holy Spirit. Teach these new disciples to obey all the commands I have given you. And be sure of this: I am with you always, even to the end of the age'" (Matthew 28:18–20).

Think about those words, *all authority*. This means "all power." Different people may think in different ways about ultimate power. Some picture the devastating effects of a nuclear bomb. In Florida, where I live, we think of a Category 5 hurricane and the destruction it leaves behind.

I have friends who survived Hurricane Andrew when it hit Miami in 1992. They buckled down at home and weathered the storm. Their description of what they went through could be made into a horror movie. One friend who lived in Homestead said that when he walked out of his home, almost everything around him was gone, leveled. The place was so ravaged that if you were able to go out in your car—if you still had a car—you had a hard time finding your way back because all the usual landmarks had been blown away by the wind. That's power! Needless to say, when these folks now hear in the forecast that there is a hurricane coming they hightail it out of town.

Think of the power of an erupting volcano. One of the most fascinating places on earth has to be Pompeii. The city is just a few miles away from Mount Vesuvius. In AD 79 Vesuvius erupted, burying and preserving the city and many of its inhabitants under several feet of volcanic ash and debris. Life came to a horrific, sudden halt as the volcano displayed its power.

The force of water from a flood or a tsunami is devastating. Videos show that in the powerful tsunami that hit Japan in 2011, cars floated downstream like little toy trucks. Houses were swept away and crushed. The power of moving water couldn't be stopped.

In the verses above, Jesus was reminding His disciples, "I have ultimate power!"

What if you really believed that the power of Jesus is much stronger than a nuke or a Cat 5 hurricane? Would that give you confidence? Think about this for a moment: the rushing energy of Niagara Falls is but a faint trickle, a bolt of lightning offers but a mere tingle, a towering tsunami seems like nothing more than a minute splash when compared to all the Son of God is and can do.

The Lord Jesus Christ has all authority down here, up there, and everywhere. And He is with you every moment of your life.

When a heckler or problem gets you down, you are giving that person or situation the right to blur your spiritual focus. You are allowing yourself to believe that those individuals or circumstances have more power to mess with your life than Jesus Christ, the King of the universe. That does not even make sense.

When being attacked by hecklers in your crowd, ask yourself, "Who's in charge here? Who is in control of my life?" I hope the answer is *God*. Even when you feel like your hands are tied, remember that His are free. And you are in His hands. Jesus said, "My sheep listen to my voice; I know them, and they follow me. I give them eternal life, and they will never perish. No one can snatch them away from me, for my Father has given them to me, and he is more powerful than anyone else. No one can snatch them from the Father's hand" (John 10:27–29).

Now that is some serious protection and care! So don't bite your nails to the knuckle. That never works and leaves you with odd-looking fingers. You must have complete confidence in the Lord that He is able to help you. Trust Him with your life.

In Ann Graham Lotz book *The Magnificent Obsession* she compares faith to a death-defying scene of a tight rope artist crossing over the Niagara Falls. With the fury of the raging waters beneath the artist maneuvers to successfully cross the falls to the delight of the crowd. But he is not done yet. To the people's amazement he manages to set a wheel barrel on the rope and proceeds to push through from one side to the other.

The crowd cheers! He then empties a heavy bag of sand on the wheel barrel and takes it across the falls once more. By now the people are gasping with suspense wondering what the artist is going to do next. But then he issues a challenge. He first asks the crowd if they believe he can put a person in the wheel barrel and push it across the falls. Everyone responds with a definite "Yes." Then he asks, "Who will volunteer?" But there's great silence. No one seems to believe him enough to do that.

But then one person, a little old man, steps up and says something like, "I believe you can wheel me across. I've seen what you can do. I volunteer." The little old man then gets in the wheel barrel and the two cross the fearsome waters of Niagara on a rope and a wheel barrel. Upon their safe return, and to the crazy roar of the crowd, the artist helps the little old man off the barrel.[1] That little old man's decision to volunteer is a vivid example of complete faith.

Total Surrender

The second important word, the second load of Psalm 34's double-barreled thinking, is the word *commit*. Commitment to anything is an act of the will. Being committed means you are going all in! Think of a yummy ham and eggs breakfast. The chickens participated, but the pigs were committed.

One of the great things we learn from believers who have gone before us is their commitment to God even during difficult times. Opposition does not easily rattle committed Christians.

In his book *Against The Night*, Charles Colson describes such vow of faith. He tells of what happened to Armando Valladares many years ago. He was arrested in Cuba for being an anti-communist. He was taken to the Isla de Pinos prison where criminals and his Christian friends were often executed at night. Their faith and trust in God was not easily shaken, though, their love for the Lord not quickly extinguished. Even when those believers faced death, Valladares could hear their voices of praise to God in the distance. And it was only after the sound of the cruel shooting of the firing squad that would there be silence once again in the night. [2]

When you are totally committed to the Lord, you are willing to do anything regardless of cost. In your mind there is no backing down, no giving up. Retreat and defeat are not in your vocabulary. You are in it to win it!

Trusting that the Lord is your help and being committed to Him are essential for silencing the hecklers in your crowd.

David reminds us of the Lord's response to a heart sold out to Him: "He will make your righteous reward shine like the dawn, your vindication like the noonday sun" (Psalm 37:6 NIV).

I live by the Atlantic Ocean. Often my wife and I are riding to her work when the sun is coming up on the east coast. The scene before us is usually stunning! Early in the morning as the sun is peeking, it burns into our hemisphere the colors that are created against the canvas of blue skies. This makes for a true work of art! Then, at dusk, the horizon on the other side is wowing.

Have you met a believer whose presence and demeanor wow you? You talk to this person and think, *There's something different about her!* The favor of God on His people makes such people radiant like the dawn, potent like the noonday sun.

When you are confident that this GREAT BIG GOD of ours is not only *with* you but also *for* you, you don't easily give in, give up, or give out before your heckler. It is true that the hecklers in your crowd may rattle you and temporarily discourage you. But that is as far as it should go.

Along your way hecklers will get loud and bring conflict into your life. Face the fact that there is more than a faint possibility, but a strong probability, that you will encounter hecklers in your crowd. They will question your motives, dreams, ideas, and routines. But with God on your side you can silence them.

Sometime back while my daughters were enjoying a live comedy performance at a club on a cruise ship, an obnoxious woman began to heckle the performer. The comedian had cerebral palsy and part of his routine was to poke jokes at himself. The crowd absolutely loved him! But the heckler's loud, rude comments attempted to kill his routine. The man on stage did not panic, however. Like a skillful mechanic dismantling a sputtering engine, the comedian took this woman's heckling apart one comment at a time. He then managed to turn the tables on her. He asked her husband about her embarrassing drinking problem. With his every rebuttal to her heckling the crowd roared with laughter until she exited the room. That comedian had successfully silenced his heckler. You can do the same!

People and unfavorable circumstances will try to dampen your passion. Don't you dare let them!

Call 'Em By Name

I'm sure that by now the names of the hecklers in your crowd, the faces of those who have turned against you, and details of the circumstances road-blocking your path to success are popping into your mind like bingo balls going up the shoot ready to be called out.

Recognizing who your hecklers are, I believe, is a critical first step to silencing them and freeing yourself from them.

If Roman Emperor Julius Caesar had been able to recognize the hecklers in his crowd (his Senate and his "friend" Brutus), things might have turned out differently for him. Sixty senators were planning to assassinate their leader. The fascinating thing about the story is that Calpurnia, Caesar's wife, had heard certain rumors about it and tried to keep him from going to the Senate meeting that day. His doctors also advised him not go. But for one reason or another, maybe pride or ego or both, Julius Caesar was blind to those who did not like him. Ironically, he rejected the warnings of those who cared for him but accepted the advice of those who secretly plotted to kill him.

Calpurnia, who sensed that there was something definitely wrong going on, begged her husband not to go. But Brutus insisted that Julius go and meet with the Senate because they had been asking for his presence. In today's vernacular Brutus must have said something like, "You've got to be kidding me, Julius. You, the powerful Caesar of Rome, is going to listen to the silly intuitions and dreams of a woman? Let's go quickly to the Senate." Caesar listened to his friend and they went. The rest is history.

Caesar's conspirators had daggers hidden within their togas. At the right moment they violently struck him. Julius Caesar was stabbed twenty-three times before he breathed his last, and his body was left there for hours before three slaves carried it to his wife.

Pinpoint the hecklers and stressors in your life! You may have a "friendly" Brutus in your crowd; hopefully no daggers or togas are involved. Keep in mind that sometimes your hecklers may not be the high-maintenance people in your life.

Sometimes hecklers are people you trust a lot. People who are close to you will, at times, turn against you. Unfortunately it has happened to me many times, even at church! Keep your spiritual eyes open. And remember that with God on your side others don't stand a chance. It is the reason the apostle Paul asked the question, "If God is for us, who can be against us?" (Romans 8:31b NIV).

One more thing: When you are hurting because of what has been said or done against you, keep in mind that every new day offers new opportunities and possibilities worth getting out of bed for. David, described in the Bible as a man after God's own heart, once wrote this bit of good news, "Weeping may last through the night, but joy comes with the morning" (Psalm 30:5b).

In other words, the density of darkness has to give way to radiant beams of sunlight. That is the day-to-day wonderful cycle God created. Birds welcome the morning with a song and there is freshness all over from the dew on the ground.

Look forward to every morning with expectation!

The first night my then-14-year-old daughter Amanda and I spent deep in a South American jungle is unforgettable. I was there with a team of close friends to preach a conference for the indigenous people who lived along the Chapare River in Bolivia.

I could not see my hand in front of my face. We were inside a mosquito net but could still hear the noises of bugs and tiny creatures. That was one long night, but our joy came in the morning when the sun broke through.

Joy is a Hebrew word that describes a ringing cry, a shout like, "YES! Made it through the night!"

Pair that thought with what the prophet Jeremiah wrote in the Old Testament book of Lamentations. Lamentations are mournful sighs from a heavy-hearted prophet. However, he was not about to let himself sink into despair because of the hecklers in his crowd. He wrote, "Yet I still dare to hope when I remember this: the faithful love of the Lord never ends! His mercies never cease. Great is his faithfulness; his mercies begin afresh each morning. I say to myself, "The Lord is my inheritance; therefore, I will hope in him!" The Lord is good to those who depend on him, to those who search for him. So it is good to wait quietly for salvation from the Lord" (Lamentations 3:21–26).

Whatever you are facing, your hope needs to be not in what you can do but in what God can do to silence your hecklers. Let the Lord rise to your rescue and quiet them, whoever they may be. That's how you overcome!

What's Your Take?

1. Imagine you were the pastor when Mr. G. started heckling you. What would you have done in that situation?
2. Describe a time in your life when you felt like you had a heckler in your crowd. This could have been a difficult person you had to deal with or a frustrating situation in your life.

3. Describe a time when you were caught by surprise. (This doesn't necessarily have to do with a heckler; it could be any time, funny or not, when something happened that you were not expecting.)

4. Read John 10:27–29: "My sheep listen to my voice; I know them, and they follow me. I give them eternal life, and they will never perish. No one can snatch them away from me, for my Father has given them to me, and he is more powerful than anyone else. No one can snatch them from the Father's hand."

5. Exercise: Put a coin in your hand and have someone in the group try to open your hand to get it. The point of the exercise is that Jesus Christ will never let you go.

6. Read Romans 8:38–39 NIV: "For I am convinced that neither death nor life, neither angels nor demons, neither the present nor the future, nor any powers, neither height nor depth, nor anything else in all creation, will be able to separate us from the love of God that is in Christ Jesus our Lord." Use one-word answers to describe how these verses make you feel and why. (Possible answers can be secure, relieved, happy, loved, or empowered.)

2

Haters Among Us

*People who know you love you, hate you, or can
do without you. Relish the former, forget the
latter, and beware of the ones in the middle.*

A HECKLER IS someone who harasses for the purpose of unsettling you and throwing you off course. Judas, for example, was a heckler in Jesus's crowd. He was one of the elite twelve and yet he turned against his Friend. He was the original Benedict Arnold. Psalm 41 describes what Judas did, "Even my best friend, the one I trusted completely, the one who shared my food, has turned against me" (Psalm 41:9).

Keep in mind that Judas spent a lot of time around Jesus. They traveled together from town to town, ate breakfast, lunch, and dinner together, and faced friends and foes as a team. Judas learned from the Master as He taught in public and lovingly explained the meaning of everything to him and the other disciples in private. Jesus had opened His heart to Judas and the rest of the men. They had laughed, dreamed, and cried together. And yet Judas betrayed the Lord.

Earlier in Psalm 41, the author gives us a little more insight into what Judas and other hecklers can be like, "They visit me as if they were my friends, but all the while they gather gossip, and when they leave, they spread it everywhere" (Psalm 41:6).

You may read those words and whisper, "I've been there. I know what that feels like." Sometimes people's compliments are hollow, empty of meaning. And although some may smile in your presence their words against you are like poisonous darts when you turn your back.

In other words, you assume hecklers are for you and with you and yet all they are doing while by your side is gathering whatever firepower they can to try to take you down later. They are pretenders with a malicious agenda!

I usually visualize a heckler as an obnoxiously loud pipsqueak in an audience who makes idiotic remarks for the purpose of frustrating the artist on stage. Hecklers make you feel bad.

In a lifetime you'll be able to count with one hand how many close intimate friends you've had. In contrast, you will have an abundance of friends and acquaintances. The sad reality is that some of them will not have your best interest in mind and may become potential hecklers in your life.

You would never dream of finding hecklers (referred to as *haters* for the rest of this chapter) among friends, family, and acquaintances, but it happens.

Susan (not her real name) is a middle aged woman I know who grew up with loving parents. Her mom and dad were sharp-minded professionals who provided a Christian home for her. When Susan was a teenager she went through a rebellious stage. She wore black clothes, had the typical flare of bad attitude, and was hanging out with like-minded characters. Then a hater appeared in an unexpected place, her high school classroom. Teachers are supposed to be encouragers, not discouragers, the wind beneath one's wings, if you may. But one day a frustrated teacher told Susan she would never amount to anything in life.

Unfortunately the teacher's words hit a target deep in Susan's subconscious mind. Someone said that while a knife wound heals, a heart wound doesn't. Believing the hater's words, Susan eventually dropped out of school and ran away from home. Her parents were devastated! They looked everywhere for her and, thankfully, finally found her, brought her home, encouraged her, and loved her unconditionally.

With God's help, Susan turned around and eventually earned her high school GED. She subsequently enrolled in college, fell in love, and got married. It seemed like a fairy tale story with a happy ending, but Susan's honeymoon didn't last long.

Her husband, the love of her life, became another hater in her life. He became verbally and physically abusive and, once again, Susan found herself in a living hell. The divorce couldn't come soon enough. Susan was heartbroken. The hater's voice of her past that had been silent for so many years came to life like a sleeping giant. Doubts once again laid siege to her mind. Would she ever amount to anything worthwhile?

It was decision time for Susan! She could either allow herself to go on a downward spiral or set a new course forward. Fortunately she chose to press on and turn things around and never look back! Eventually she met a loving young man who accepted her, loved her, and eventually married her. Susan also went back to school. A doctor's degree now hangs on a wall at her office. She had silenced her haters and proved them wrong!

One way to silence a hater in your life is to turn his/her negative, frustrating words into fuel that fires your passion to succeed. Make haters your motivation to press forward to a better life.

Owning It

You may not see it, but lying beneath the surface of who you are is a lot of precious raw material. God has equipped you and is waiting for the opportunity to use you! The Lord has loaded you up with abilities and talents you can tap into. He wove a purpose into the fabric of your being. The Lord also loaded you up with abilities and talents to help you succeed in life. Consider the following amazing account of David's creation a part of your own biography, "You made my whole being; you formed me in my mother's body. I praise you because you made me in an amazing and wonderful way. What you have done is wonderful. I know this very well. You saw my bones being formed as I took shape in my mother's body. When I was put together there, you saw my body as it was formed. All the days planned for me were written in your book before I was one day old" (Psalm 139:13–16 NCV).

There is a certain spiritual discipline called *praying the Scriptures*. The idea is to read something in the Bible, claim it as your own, and pray the words back to God as if reminding Him of the words He once inspired.

I challenge you to make the following a prayer to God, "Lord, You made my whole being; You formed me, (your full name), perfectly in my mother's womb. I praise You for making me just the way I am. What You did is wonderful! I am wonderful because of You!! When You were putting me together inside my mom's womb You were watching me and loving me. You have a perfect plan for me. You wrote the story of my life in your book before I was even born. Thank You for loving me so. I love You, Lord." PLEASE READ THAT AGAIN SLOWLY.

When you pray the Scriptures, you are agreeing with God about what He says and thinks. Let what God has inspired inspire you!

I came up with a short list of abilities and personality traits. If they describe you, they should make you feel extremely special. Please find a pen or pencil and put a check mark next to those qualities you believe you possess:

Creativity and thinking outside the box
A contagious smile
A magnetic personality (people gravitate toward you)
The ability to work well with numbers and/or words
The ability to work well with computers and/or electronics
Being quick on your feet
Having a great voice or ability to play a musical instrument well
Having a great palate and a passion for cooking
Writing stories or expressing your thoughts through a keyboard
A love for animals
Giving of yourself to help others
Working well with your hands
A green thumb
Knowledge of how things work and the ability to fix them
Other: (please write down any other qualities you have)

Of course, this is just a short list to get the juices in your brain flowing. I challenge you to also jot down other ideas of what makes you special. Hopefully you will run out of paper. I am talking about those things that motivate you and come easy for you. Those very things, when properly used, can catapult you forward!

BUT WAIT!

PRAY before you start thinking and writing!

This is essential. Ask the Lord to bring to mind how He has accessorized you, every detail He included when He was assembling you in your mother's womb. Please do not easily give up if you are having a hard time getting started. Please do not be too hard on yourself. God thinks there's a lot of you to love! First think of three words that describe you as a person. Once you are done with those three, write down five more. As you gain momentum and get on a roll, keep writing, and then write some more.

Time to Turn the Tables

Decide in your heart that there is much about yourself to be thankful for. Commit yourself to sharpening your strengths while turning the negatives in your life into positives.

In my early days as the pastor-teacher of an Anglo church I became very conscious of my Spanish accent when I listened to a sermon I had preached. I was not aware of such a thing until I heard myself. I was devastated. I felt like a failure. I had worked so hard to command the English language, but the accent stuck to me like glue. Then someone told me that I looked like Fez in *That '70s Show* and sounded like Ricky Ricardo in *I Love Lucy*. I really had issues with sounding like English is my second language (even though it is).

But then the Holy Spirit used my darling wife and a few close friends to help me see that the accent could be a strength in ministry rather than a weakness. I began to realize that many listeners like the way accents sound. Beyond that, when I speak some people have to really pay attention; otherwise, they will whisper to their neighbor, "What did he just say?" I was able to turn what I thought was a negative into a positive.

Do the same with whatever holds you back. Make what your hecklers say and do a vivid reminder of the goals you are moving toward. View your opinionated pundits as the very people you need to succeed!

Like Susan, you may face a critical crossroad to either yield to haters' voices against you or shut them up and move past them once and for all. My hope is for you to rise above the people and circumstances that put you down and slow you down.

Sometimes people and bad circumstances make us lose track of how precious we really are in the eyes of God. Some are able to overcome these right away while others take years to find themselves and their worth and get back on track. Jean's story reminds us not to give up hope.

Duncan MacLeod gave his bride, Jean, a twenty-two-karat gold ring to celebrate their wedding. One day, while Jean was helping her mom gather some corn out in the field, the ring slipped off her finger and she lost it. She was broken hearted and spent the whole day crying and looking for her precious ring. Duncan came back from serving in the Air Force and bought her another ring, but it just wasn't the same.

Fifty-five years later Jean saw a man named Eric Soane using a metal detector in the field where the ring had been lost long before. She told him the story and challenged him to find it. Two hours later Eric had the ring in his hands. He found it buried six inches deep in the ground and dug it up. Can you imagine? Jean never lost hope of finding the ring. It just took over fifty years to get it.[3]

In the Sound Booth

In the last chapter you identified the hecklers in your life. Now let's fine-tune the art of silencing hecklers/haters by diagnosing what they sound like.

Some years ago after taking a shower I was using a Q-tip to clean the outside of my right ear. While doing that, I was using my left ear to listen to messages on my phone. Then the phone slipped from my left hand and instinctively my right hand went to reach for it. As a result I put the Q-tip through my right eardrum. I looked like Frankenstein with a stick coming out of my ear! Man, that was that painful!

Several visits and ear examinations followed in a room I called the *torture chamber*. One of the tests I was subjected to happened in a booth inside a soundproof room. The audiologist gave me headphones to wear and played sounds and frequencies for me to listen to in each of my ears. Some were loud while others soft. Every time I recognized a sound I would signal it by raising either my right or left hand, depending on which ear I was hearing the sound through. After the test was over the audiologist determined my degree of hearing loss.

Just like I had to be able to recognize the various sounds coming through those headphones, we need to be able to pick out what haters sound like. Their words are replayed in our minds over and over like bad reruns: *you're not that smart; you got what you deserved; you have too little willpower; you will likely fail; no one likes you, that's why you don't have friends; God doesn't have any use for you; who do you think you are? You are never going to amount to anything.* A clear-cut mark of a hater is that he/she makes us think less of ourselves.

Counteract the nauseating sound of those words by whispering positive phrases to yourself, such as, *"I can," "I am able," "I'm smart," "I do have what it takes," "I will not stop until I get there," "I look sharp," "I'm pretty,"* and *"I am wonderfully made, Lord; you made me amazingly."*

Point at the image of yourself in the mirror and say, "You're alright!"

Our greatest battles are won in the recesses of our minds!

The apostle Paul wrote this great truth: "We destroy people's arguments and every proud thing that raises itself against the knowledge of God. We capture every thought and make it give up and obey Christ" (2Corinthians 10:4b–5 NCV).

What a great idea! I have committed that last statement to memory. The Lord uses it often to get my mind back on track when it wanders off in the wrong direction. By the way, those are not magic words. Paul was referring to a spiritual war that is won by faith and through the daily surrendering of self to the Holy Spirit and His overcoming power. Learn to live by that thought.

My brother Hector, who is now in heaven, was an extremely successful businessman. He worked both hard and smart and provided a great life for his family. Hector believed that all things are possible when God is at your side (Matthew 19:26). When a meeting went well or when others favored him, he would say something like, "I am God's favorite person!" What a fantastic attitude to have. Do you see yourself in that light? Do you give yourself the thumbs up?

STOP READING and say out loud, "I am God's favorite person!"

Did you do it? Successful actions are a result of positive and purposeful thought processes. Stay humble yet positive about your life. Always remember that God is the author of your success. The wise proverb goes, "Be careful what you think, because your thoughts run your life" (Proverbs 4:23 NCV).

We should store the good times in our hearts and keep them under lock and key. Give God control of your mind and heart! Then once He recalibrates your brain, refuse to allow haters to break your spirit. Don't let their words take root in your heart.

Your heart belongs to Jesus. Haters' words and deeds are like weeds growing in a beautiful garden God is trying to create in your heart. Pull that junk out!

Friend or Foe?

You may be familiar with the Old Testament story of Job. He was a man who faced a series of very unfortunate events. In one sorry, no-good day, Job lost his property, servants, and almost all he owned. Soon thereafter his ten children died at the same time during a freak accident. They were having a family reunion when something like an F-5 tornado ripped through the place. Job had lost everything he considered precious except for his wife. To add insult to injury, Job got sick with nasty, festering boils and sores all over his body.

Needless to say the man was feeling pretty lousy. Then three of his "friends" showed up at his door and became haters. They kicked him while he was down (not literally of course), saying that he got what he deserved. Instead of pulling Job up they pushed him down deeper into despair.

I am blessed to have a few friends that remind me of the joys of my life when I have forgotten what those are. I'm sure you do as well. I challenge you to get in touch with them today. Call them, text them, email them, Instagram them, or Tweet them and let them know how special they are.

A friend becomes a hater, however, when he/she regularly and vindictively points out your flaws and imperfections (as if you didn't already know what those are). I have an older friend who told me his buddies used to call him "Snoz" because of his big nose. With friends like that, who needs enemies? The funny thing is that I had never paid attention to his nose until he pointed it out; actually, it's not that big anyway. I am just suggesting that you recognize a hater when you hear one.

When referring to the devil, the Christian's enemy, the Lord Jesus said, "The thief's purpose is to steal and kill and destroy." (John 10:10a)

Although all of us are inherently sinful imperfect beings who often lean toward wrong-doing (Psalm 51:5), the evil one uses people in our lives to make us trip, fall, and get hurt. Satan was the author of Job's drama and trauma. He was also the mastermind behind Judas' wretched plan to betray Jesus (Luke 22:3–4) and the one causing Peter to tempt Jesus to abandon His purpose of going to Jerusalem to die on the cross for the sins of the world (Matthew 16:21–23). In that last Bible passage, Jesus called Peter a stumbling block. The Greek word for *stumbling block* is from the root where we get our English word *scandal*.

Scandals usually have to do with some kind of misconduct. They often result in shame and embarrassment to someone. Maybe the haters in your life are urging you to do something that can potentially bring you down spiritually, morally, emotionally, and in every other way possible. Recognize their tune and refuse to dance to it.

Before I close this chapter, let me just point out that sometimes people you know just come across wrong but have no ill will toward you. No malicious intent. Friends may say the wrong thing at the wrong time. It hurts, but you do not hold it permanently against them because you know that is not their intention. I said the wrong thing to an acquaintance from India not long ago, but he did not hold it against me.

Just before Thanksgiving he told me that in his home they celebrate the holiday but without eating turkey. Their religious beliefs forbid them from eating any kind of meat. As we talked some more he said something that really surprised me, and without thinking I said, "HOLY COW!" Immediately my inner voice screamed something like, *Are you serious? Think before you speak, man.* As he kept talking he told me his religion is Hindu. He also said that cows are considered sacred and that many people honor them by praying to them. Again, with no intention of being a hater and with a silly grin in my face I said, "You all pray to a cow for real?" But he just looked at me. At this time the mini-me in my brain screamed, *Shut your mouth, idiot, and get out of here!*

It wasn't my intention to offend him in any way, but it sure sounded like it. Friends do that sometimes. A hater takes jabs at you often, with the purpose of hurting you.

A healthy self-confidence can help you accomplish a lot and move forward. But keep in mind that there are limitations and dangers to thinking you can do all you want on your own.

Even mighty people fall. Superman had kryptonite, Achilles had a weak heel, and Iron Man is nothing without his suit. People who trust only in themselves ultimately end up frustrated. Your faith needs to be in the One who is limitless. You have boundaries. He does not. He owns the cattle on a thousand hills! (Psalm 50:10). You may have decent ideas. His are mind blowing!

Simply put, instead of being self-confident, be God-confident.

Faith is confidence that defies the odds!

I shared with you earlier that my brother passed away a few short years ago. I miss him dearly. Hector always had an incredible talent to do anything he set his mind to. From business, to electronics, to figuring out life's problems, he seemed to always succeed. Hector believed his Savior and Creator favored him. He had fully embraced what the prophet said, "'For I know the plans I have for you,' declares the Lord, 'plans to prosper you and not to harm you, plans to give you hope and a future'" Jeremiah 29:11 (NIV). This verse is also tattooed on the rib cage of a good friend of mine.

There may be haters among you who will try to disrupt your life, but the Lord in you will help you prevail. Ask Susan, Jean, Job, Hector (when you get to Heaven), or anyone for whom God has come through.

By the way, when Job's tough times were over God gave him more beautiful children. He became wealthier than he had ever been and he fully enjoyed the rest of his days on earth! There may be haters among you, but they will ultimately fade away as you recognize their familiar song and tune them out of your mind.

What's Your Take?

1. Name a person in your life whom you would not think would become a heckler. (Possible answers could be: my boss, my parents, my good neighbor, my best friend, my trainer/coach, or my church leaders.)

2. The author told a story of a time when he put a Q-tip through his ear. Have you ever had a freak accident or has anything crazy happened to you? Explain. Or, have you ever said something that came out wrong and sounded hurtful but you meant nothing by it? Share.

3. Have you ever prayed the Scriptures? Is there a specific Bible verse you use or quote when you pray? Share.

4. Jeremiah 29:11 (NIV) "For I know the plans I have for you,' declares the LORD, 'plans to prosper you and not to harm you, plans to give you hope and a future'" is a favorite for many people. Do you have a favorite verse? Which? Do you know people who have Bible verses tattooed on their bodies? Which verses?

5. Name certain qualities you have that make you special.

6. Some people have a hard time looking at themselves in the mirror and saying, "You are special!" Why would some people have a hard time recognizing how amazing they really are in God's eyes? (A possible answer could be that they have not yet accepted the total grace and love of God for them.)

PART 2

Your Secret Weapon

3

Intimidators
and Bullies

A man who is intimate with God
is not intimidated by man.

<small>Leonard Ravenhill[4]</small>

Dale Earnhardt was one of the best racecar drivers of all times. He was known as *The Intimidator*. At close to two hundred miles per hour, Earnhardt would aggressively drive his black number 3 Chevy right up the back bumper of the car in front of him in order to pass him. The sight of Earnhardt's black car in the rear view mirror put other drivers on edge. In fact the word intimidate comes from a combination of two Latin words meaning '*in fear.*'

An amusement park in Virginia has a scary ginormous roller coaster called Intimidator 305 named after Earnhardt. The coaster peaks at three-hundred-five-feet. It then takes would-be daredevils into a mega-drop that reaches an insane speed of ninety miles an hour. Quick turns, twists, and more drops follow. People have even blacked out during the ride.[5]

Intimidating circumstances and people makes us afraid and insecure. If you play sports, your opponent will use anything (a black mouthpiece, a dark visor, stares, trash talk) to intimidate and discourage you. Muhammad Ali was a master at that. Weeks before a fight he would get belligerent telling his opponents that he was the greatest. He would continue these antics all the way to the day of the bout in order to mess with his opponent's mind. He did it to gain the advantage and discourage his rival.

The word *discouragement* is synonymous with *intimidation*. Hecklers can be intimidators and discouragers who mentally try to take you apart piece by piece. The greatest intimidator/heckler of all times was a huge, tough soldier in the Philistine army named Goliath.

Jumbo Combo

One of the most beloved stories of all times is the battle between the Hebrew shepherd, David, and the Philistine giant, Goliath. Even if you never went to Sunday school, you've probably heard of the boy who went *mano a mano* with the mighty warrior. This is the mother of all Cinderella stories, as the underdog, underweight and ill-equipped David defeated the seasoned veteran killer.

According to the story, every day Goliath went on a verbal attack against King Saul of Israel and his army. With a valley separating the two enemy armies, Goliath would step out of his ranks:

"Goliath stood and shouted a taunt across to the Israelites. Why are you all coming out to fight?" he called. "I am the Philistine champion, but you are only the servants of Saul. Choose one man to come down here and fight me...I defy the armies of Israel today. Send me a man who will fight me" (1Samuel 17:8,10).

Goliath was taunting, shaming, and challenging anyone within earshot of him. Have you had someone in your life messing with your mind like that? Bullying happens every day, not only in schools but also in offices, locker rooms, social gatherings, and social media.

Everywhere. Antagonists will try to push you around mentally and physically in an effort to run over you and take advantage of you. Their goal is to excel at your expense.

Even moments before his battle against David, Goliath was trying to crawl into David's mind to intimidate him: "Goliath walked out toward David with his shield bearer ahead of him, sneering in contempt at this ruddy-faced boy. 'Am I a dog,' he roared at David, 'that you come at me with a stick?' And he cursed David by the names of his gods. 'Come over here, and I'll give your flesh to the birds and wild animals!' Goliath yelled" (1Samuel 17:41–44).

Words can be paralyzing! Like the thief who broke into a Christian lady's house not knowing she was in there. She quietly watched him and then yelled, "Stop, thief! Acts 2:44." At those words the thief stopped and surrendered. When the arresting officer asked the man why he stopped, the thief answered, "I thought she said she had an ax and two .44's."

Goliath was harassing David, but that didn't stop the little guy from charging at him. In fact, David had already dealt with heckling in his own camp. This part of the story you may not know offhand.

One of David's brothers, a soldier in the Hebrew army, had been verbally undermining David. According to the written record, David had just arrived at the battle site when he heard Goliath spit out his poison against Israel. David couldn't believe how scared everyone was at the sight of the giant. David was confident that by faith he could put a beat-down on Goliath. In his mind, the Philistine champ was nothing but a chump!

So David started asking the soldiers around him about the reward for anyone willing to fight and kill Goliath. He was told the winner would get the king's daughter's hand in marriage and his family would be exempt from taxes forever. BAM! That sealed the deal in

David's mind! In his heart he accepted the challenge and was willing to take on the battle royal.

Have you ever gotten really excited about something that had the potential of being great? You were running on pure adrenaline and couldn't stop thinking about all the possibilities and what-ifs. But you were stopped in your tracks by a heckler. Hecklers have the uncanny ability to bring you down from the clouds. Nauseating, isn't it?

David was pumped about the exciting idea of beating Goliath. Thinking about the cute princess brought chills down his spine. And not paying taxes sounded pretty sweet. But then David's brother became a heckler in his crowd. Check out what the Bible says, "But when David's oldest brother, Eliab, heard David talking to the men, he was angry. 'What are you doing around here anyway?' he demanded. 'What about those few sheep you're supposed to be taking care of? I know about your pride and deceit. You just want to see the battle!' 'What have I done now?' David replied. 'I was only asking a question!'" (1Samuel 17:28–29)

Stop and think about that for a moment. Eliab was belittling, devaluing, and humiliating David in front of others. Talk about having to battle a jumbo combo. Not only was the intimidating Goliath looming on David's horizon, he also had to deal with his own brother's insults. David could have gotten his feelings hurt and gone home, but he didn't.

By the way, if you're a very sensitive person, you are going to have a hard time with hecklers. They pounce when they sense they're getting to you. Never show hecklers that they are getting under your skin.

When a heckler puts you down in order to slow you down, never give him/her the satisfaction of seeing you sweat.

Long ago someone advised me to be turtle-like, hard shell on the outside but soft inside. Turtle-like people show a tough exterior.

Negative criticism bounces off them like bullets do off the Hulk. But on the inside they keep a kind, compassionate heart.

David heard Eliab's heckling but kept going without missing a step. His was a three-headed goal: become a giant slayer, kiss and marry the princess, and get a lifetime pass from taxes. That is exactly what happened and more. David won the battle, gained much fame, married the girl, and became king of Israel, thus being tax-exempt for life.

The Lord Who Bursts Through...

Moving rapidly into the battlefield, the shepherd boy found a few smooth stones, put one in his slingshot and launched it in the direction of the Philistine warrior. The stone hit the big man square on the forehead, and, as if pressed by the invisible giant finger of God, sank in place, knocking Goliath unconscious. David ran towards him and cut Goliath's head off. The Bible does not tell us, but I wonder if David lifted the severed head up by the hair, shook it, and let out a big "YEAH" as he performed some sort of Old Testament end zone dance. It must have been a magical moment, a top ten in the history of battles! I hope there's a 3-D VR video of that in Heaven. Now check out what happened later, "So David...defeated the Philistines there. 'The LORD did it!' David exclaimed. 'He burst through my enemies like a raging flood!' So he named that place Baal-perazim (which means "the Lord who bursts through")" (2Samuel 5:20).

The Lord who bursts through! I like that!

How about fully believing that the God you worship today is the same exact God David worshipped? The same Lord who helped David will also help you. He is your secret weapon. When facing your intimidating, bullying, undermining hecklers, believe God will burst through their words and plans against you.

Some time back thieves drilled a hole into the six-foot-thick re-inforced concrete vault wall of the Hatton Garden Safe Deposit in London. They opened many safety deposit boxes and got away with what would be comparable to as much as $300 million (American) in jewelry. Wow! They burst through and robbed.[6]

When God Almighty bursts through for you, He is there to make a deposit into your life's account, not to take anything away. He gives you peace, freedom, presence of mind, and whatever you need so you may live in victory. Faith in the Lord of Heaven is the key that un-locks God's amazing blessing for you—spiritual or physical or both.

I challenge you to, like David, have the faith-mind that God will fight your battles for you. In the showdown between David and Goliath, David's answer to the giant's threats and intimidation was simple but accurate, "David replied to the Philistine, 'You come to me with sword, spear, and javelin, but I come to you in the name of the LORD of Heaven's Armies—the God of the armies of Israel, whom you have defied. Today the LORD will conquer you, and I will kill you and cut off your head. And then I will give the dead bodies of your men to the birds and wild animals, and the whole world will know that there is a God in Israel!'" (1Samuel 17:45–46)

It's interesting that even though it was David who did the work of conquering, killing, and cutting off Goliath's head, he attributed the victory to God. David was like the Super Bowl MVP who said, "First of all I want to thank my Lord and Savior Jesus Christ for giving me the ability to help the team win. Without Him I wouldn't be here."

David told the giant: "The Lord will conquer, kill, and cut off your head." God was the One who did it but He used David's quick-ness, strategy, slingshot-throwing accuracy, and arm strength to sever the head.

The Lord will use everything about you—your education, street smarts, common sense, experience, skill set, and thought process—to hand you the victory. It is His accomplishment and He wants to get the glory for it, but God lets you share in the fun by allowing you to do what is required for victory.

In another Bible story, when King Jehoshaphat of Judah and his men were facing a jumbo combo of three powerful armies, the king was terrified. He turned to God and prayed a desperation prayer. A small part of it went like this, "O our God, won't you stop them? We are powerless against this mighty army that is about to attack us. We do not know what to do, but we are looking to you for help" (2Chronicles 20:12).

I have been there with Jehoshaphat, my back against the wall with nowhere to turn. I'm sure you have too. But then the Lord comes through in a miraculous way. The Lord inspired one of Jehoshaphat's men, Jahaziel, to say this, "Listen, all you people of Judah and Jerusalem! Listen, King Jehoshaphat! This is what the LORD says: 'Do not be afraid! Don't be discouraged by this mighty army, for the battle is not yours, but God's'" (2Chronicles 20:15).

Whenever you feel threatened because of the difficulties before you, PRAY! Then remember those seven most powerful words, THE BATTLE IS NOT YOURS, BUT GOD'S!

A teenager said something insightful to me not long ago, "When you work, you work, but when you pray, God works!" Let the Lord work out your heckler situation and give Him the glory for it.

I am convinced that the heavenly spotlight was shining on young David because he was the only one around willing to stand for God.

You may be the only one in your office or among your neighbors or friends who is a believer. Stand for God! Not in an aggressive Bible-thumping kind of way, but in a kind yet resolute way. When the name of the Lord you serve is put into question, do not be afraid to state your convictions. Be counted like David.

When I was in college I played in a tennis doubles tournament. My partner was another college student. He was a good tennis player but had a foul mouth. He cursed a lot, especially when we lost a point. Early in the tourney I pulled him aside and told him I did not appreciate him taking the Lord's name in vain. He apologized and told me he would try not to curse that way.

Next game my partner did it again. He missed a shot at the net and used Jesus's name in vain. I yelled back, "Jesus didn't missed the shot, brah, you did!" Later he did it again but this time instead of Jesus, he gave God a last name. I immediately yelled back, "Don't bring God into this; He's not the one playing!" My partner looked back at me and said, "I'm sorry, man. I forget you don't like it." From then on, any time poison was spewed from his lips he would look at me and say, "Sorry" or "My bad." Eventually he completely stopped cursing when we played and in the end we won the tournament.

The point is that we, the family of God, need to be bold for God and trust Him. Making a faith-stand for the Lord puts us at the edge of greatness in His overcoming kingdom.

One way of bolstering your faith is to go back in your mind (or journal) to your experiences with God and remember how He has come through for you time and again. Think of the answered prayers you've had, the miracles you've enjoyed, heard about, and read of, and all that the Lord has helped you overcome in years past.

Tomorrow's victories often come from yesterday's triumphs and today's efforts.

That's what David did in preparation for the battle. King Saul was not sure of the young shepherd's ability to fight Goliath, "But David persisted. 'I have been taking care of my father's sheep and goats,' he said. 'When a lion or a bear comes to steal a lamb from the flock, I go after it with a club and rescue the lamb from its mouth.

If the animal turns on me, I catch it by the jaw and club it to death. I have done this to both lions and bears, and I'll do it to this pagan Philistine, too, for he has defied the armies of the living God! The LORD who rescued me from the claws of the lion and the bear will rescue me from this Philistine!'" (1Samuel 17:34–37)

David's reasoning has to become your own. Grow and learn from your experiences of the past, good and bad. Then deal confidently with your heckler, knowing that as God has helped you in the past He will do so again in the present.

The author of the book of Hebrews reminds us that, "Jesus Christ is the same yesterday, today, and forever" (Hebrews 13:8).

Past victories empower us for facing and overcoming present and future battles. Your experiences are an invaluable source of training and wisdom. Lay them before God and use them to plow through intimidating circumstances and people.

One more thought: like David, stay focused on your goals. The young man didn't let Eliab's put-down or Goliath's intimidating threats slow him down from getting the giant, the girl, and the gold. You too must keep your eyes on the prize.

When I was in college I was crazy about telling others about Jesus. I would even go into the men's bathroom, unroll the toilet paper in the stalls, and roll them back up while inserting Gospel tracts after three or four squares. I would do that in prominent places, such as where I knew the university president would go use the rest room.

One time I witnessed to a young man in the cafeteria, and he not only rejected what I had to say but also told me he was a Satan worshipper. I thanked him for his time and went on. That young man began to stalk me, showing up at my classes. He would follow me around school. Then one day he stopped me and told me that their group had put a curse on me to get seriously hurt and die. He grabbed my shoulders and said, "Look into my eyes." His eyes looked red as fire and his pupils moved rapidly from one corner of his eyes to the other. I had never seen anything like it before. I felt weak at the knees while he smiled and said, "You thought I was joking." As he walked away, I was petrified. Scared. Bullied. I had an evil heckler in my crowd.

That afternoon the secretary I worked for in the school's student work program told me a parable Jesus taught about Him being stronger than our enemy. She encouraged me, a young believer, to be strong in the Lord.

That night I went to the house of one of the elders of my church for guidance. Using slightly different words than the secretary's, he shared the same ideas with me. He reminded me of how the Lord Jesus had saved me and is always with me. He added that I needed to get on my knees and pray in the name and the power of Jesus's blood, asking God to break the curse. And I did.

The next day the young man did not show up to any of my classes. I didn't see him for a solid week. Then one day while I was sitting in the hallway waiting for my next class, he showed up. He said, "I just came by to tell you that there's not a curse on you anymore. I don't know what happened but…" I was so excited I interrupted him and wanted to hug him but he argued, "Don't touch me. I can't allow you to touch me." And that was the end of that. God had fought the battle, gotten the victory, and silenced my heckler. All I had to do was keep my eyes on Him.

After that experience I went on sharing my faith on campus.

This is how you silence your hecklers and overcome: by having faith that God will burst through for you, remembering your past experiences, and staying focused on your goals!

What's Your Take?

1. Begin the session by discussing the scariest, most intimidating roller coaster rides the group members have been on.
2. Discuss the last time anyone heard trash-talking going on at a sporting event, in the office, or at a family gathering. How did the person being trashed respond?
3. David named the place where God gave him the victory "Baal-perazim" or "The Lord who bursts through." Have individuals in the group share times when they felt the Lord busted through a difficult situation for them.
4. Past experiences can be extremely valuable to tackle present troubles. Would anyone in the group be willing to share a helpful life experience? Life experiences may cover a wide range of topics: dealing with a loved one who is fighting cancer, how a person went about finding a great job, successfully losing weight, overcoming a certain fear or addiction, overcoming the death of a loved one, overcoming divorce and being single and happy again, and many others.
5. Discuss why it seems so difficult to stand for God among family, friends, work, or social gatherings.

4

The Heckler of Facts

The only thing worse than being blind
is having sight and no vision.

HELEN KELLER[7]

IN THE BOOK To Dream Again Robert Dale tells of a day when Pooh
and Piglet were talking. Piglet asked Pooh what he thought about
whenever he got up in the morning. Pooh, always thinking with his
belly, spoke of whatever yummy food he could eat first. Pooh then
asked Piglet the same question and Piglet answered, "I say, 'I wonder
what exciting thing is going to happen today.'"[8]

Wouldn't it be great to dream big dreams? When Walter Disney
came up with his idea for Disneyland not a lot of people could visualize what he saw. Outside of Los Angeles, where he wanted to build,
there was nothing but undeveloped land. But Walt could see beyond
the trees and brush. He could see a majestic castle and a people mover
overhead and families laughing and spinning madly around in giant
teacups.

Walt Disney had it all mapped out in his mind. There may have
been cows gracing on some spot among the citrus trees in that huge
piece of land but to Disney that cattle was right where Frontierland

would one day be (or Fantasyland or Tomorrowland or Main Street USA or where a Mississippi paddle boat would be floating). It wasn't going to be easy for Disney, though. What stood between him and his dreams were many acres of rural land and lack of funds. Those kinds of odds could have sunk anyone, but not Disney.

He drew images of the place for others to see and began sharing his vision with the world. Many caught the vision and today Disneyland is one of the top vacation destinations of the world.

You too have the power to plant a vision in others!

Imagine a dad drawing word pictures in the mind of his little girl: "You are going to go far in life. I believe in you. You're so smart and talented that nothing's going to be able to hold you back." And then as she joins the work force he keeps drawing: "Girl, I don't just see you working for that company; you're going to own the place one day. Your name is going to be on their sign." His daughter is empowered to succeed.

The Lord validates us as well. He inspired the apostle Paul to write: "For we are God's masterpiece. He has created us anew in Christ Jesus, so we can do the good things he planned for us long ago" (Ephesians 2:10).

The word *masterpiece* in Greek means *poem*. In God's eyes, believers are rhythmic and flowing and composed in a way that is beautiful to behold.

When I think of a masterpiece, a few pictures come to mind: The majestic Taj Mahal, the amazing Sistine Chapel, the Mona Lisa, Michelangelo's Pieta sculpture. The detail in those works of art is mind-blowing.

None of those can compare to the awesomeness of how God made you. You are His best creation. You are the Lord's most prized work of art.

I challenge you right now to STOP READING, look at your image in the mirror, point and say, "You are a real masterpiece!" Did you do it? C'mon, try it.

Internalizing how God thinks about you can help push you past the heckler of facts. God has your best interest in mind and wants to do great things in and through you. The challenge in this chapter is for you to start dreaming and do it big.

Clear Vision

Facts have a tendency of clouding our vision. For many of us they are a constant reminder that life is not as you once pictured it would be. The facts of failed relationships, illness, unemployment, a criminal record, single parenting, age, unfulfilled dreams and many more can ruin a perfectly good day. Discouragement may start small but can take over our whole being. A negative thought, when not dealt with, can make you a basket case of emotions. When that is allowed to continue, it puts you into a state of depression.

I noticed one morning recently that a little corner of a dry, clean dishtowel I had put by the kitchen sink had fallen into a bowl filled with water in the sink. But I thought nothing of it. When I came back home for lunch the moisture had gone up the towel so that half of it was wet. Typical male that I am, I left it there. When I returned home after work I glanced at it again. By then the whole towel was soaked. Through whatever laws of physics are involved, the moisture had continued creeping up the dry towel. What started as a dry towel ended as a sopping mess.

Consider that the small negative facts of your present life have the potential of putting a big damper on your fire. Worse, you may be thinking: *life is what it is and there's little chance of changing that.* That's the heckler of facts talking, not God.

Twenty days after my bride and I said, "I do" at the altar, we packed up all our belongings into our Pontiac Sunbird and headed for graduate school in New Orleans. Doreen was nineteen years old and I was twenty-four. Upon graduation I got my first full time job as a pastor of a church in the mountains of New Mexico. Life wasn't easy there and it snowed like crazy. I remember losing a key in our snow-covered driveway one afternoon and not being able to find it until months later when the snow finally melted.

We may have lived in Taos, New Mexico, but our sights were on one day moving back to Florida near our parents and other relatives. The facts, however, were against that happening; we were far from the Sunshine State, my resume was one among many of pastors wanting to move to Florida, our finances were extremely tight, I was young and had little experience, the congregation I was serving was in a re-mote location, I had no influence or much contact with anyone back home (those were the days before social media), and me, a Hispanic, trying to find an Anglo church to lead was a very unlikely scenario.

There were so many factors blocking the way to our dreams it was discouraging. All we could do was keep the vision alive, talk it up, and pray to God whose influence goes far beyond ours. God has clout!

Then one day a central Florida church called to see if we were in-terested in coming back to Florida. The fascinating thing is that their letter of interest came in the mail two days before we were scheduled to fly into Orlando for Doreen's brother's wedding.

We received the church's letter and questionnaire in the mail on Wednesday. That same afternoon I typed my responses on the type-writer (email had not yet been invented) and sent it back by express one-day mail so they could receive it by Thursday. Friday we arrived at her parents' house in Orlando. By the middle of Sunday afternoon, one day before I was scheduled to fly back to New Mexico, we had not heard back from the church that had contacted us and assumed they were not interested. Our hearts were broken, our dreams fading quickly.

I told my darling wife, "The Lord obviously doesn't want us to move back to Florida at this time. Let's pray and totally surrender our lives to staying in Taos indefinitely until the Lord is ready to move us." We prayed with tears in our eyes but with resolute commitment to follow what the Lord wanted. Not two minutes after we had said "amen" a member of the church's pastor search committee called her mom's house asking for me.

The man told me their secretary had lost my paperwork but they had just found it. In short, they met with us a couple of hours later, everything fell into place, and we were making our way back to Florida a few short months later. The Lord had made our vision a reality. We believe the God we love and serve had everything to do with it. He dialed and put my name through to that search committee. He opened their eyes to find the misplaced paperwork. He connected us to the church in such a way that the relationship has continued to this day, twenty-nine years later.

Remember this: God is your secret weapon; when you feel like your hands are tied, His are free and able to help!

Dream Big

How big are your dreams? On a scale of one to ten, with *one* being a very small dream and *ten* being a very big dream, where would your dreams score? A wise proverb states, "Where there is no vision, the people perish" (Proverbs 29:18a KJV).

I dare you to dream big. Once a dream is born it burns in your heart and becomes your motivation, the fuel to your fire. Everyone ought to have vision for his/her life, career/salary, marriage, finances, children's lives, retirement, and others.

If you can see it with the eyes of your heart, you can reach it with the hands of your faith, hard work, determination, and perseverance. I have heard it said that you ought to pray as if everything depends on God and work as if everything depends on you.

Ask God today to give you a dream for tomorrow. Remember, lack of initiative results in indifference, dullness, and boredom. Motivational speaker Zig Ziglar once said, "If you aim at nothing you will hit it every time."[9]

I've met too many aimless people. You ask about their vision and they tell you only the sad facts of their present situation. Their words are dry, their inflection monotone, their emotions humdrum. The facts of their mundane life have become hecklers in their crowd.

Go ahead! Dream the dream, then put some feet to your dreams. In other words, get to work on it. That first step you take, however, is always the hardest one. Take my writing of this book, for example: I had been talking about it for years but never moved on it. Ideas were bouncing like pinballs in my head but I was on "tilt" mode. Frozen. Doing nothing about it.

I even attended a publishing conference, joined writing webinars, read books about writing, collected lots of notes, talked with people who had been down the path I wanted to tread on, but still did not type one word. I was overwhelmed. I was pregnant with information but delaying giving birth to this book. It was a miserable time for me. I heard the voice of God telling me, "Just write," but hesitated.

All that changed when I told a friend about my dilemma. He compared me to a famous Bible prophet by the name of Jonah. You may know the story. Jonah knew what God wanted but he ran in the opposite direction. Jonah boarded a ship and sailed away. But God caught up with the man and put the pressure on by sending a big fish to swallow Jonah alive. It wasn't until Jonah was slish-sloshing in the slop of a whale's belly that Jonah prayed and committed himself to doing what God's will. Then, when the fish vomited him close to the shore, Jonah did what God wanted.

Countdown

I felt that God had put the idea of writing in my heart, so I asked Him to help me. I blocked chunks of time here and there out of my busy schedule and started typing.

So how do you go about pursuing your God-given dreams? I think it all starts by *setting a goal*. Mine was to finish this book. What's yours? If you do not have a dream, ask the Lord to give you one.

After you know what your goal is, set a tentative date for when you want to reach it. You could even break down your goal into small stages and complete them one at a time. Setting a date can make everything official. And if you do not make your deadline, instead of getting discouraged, set another date for completion and target that. The point is to have a timeline to go by.

Then daily, regularly, infuse your spiritual dream with spiritual power. *Pray! Trust God* along the way. He will lead you. He loves you. The Lord is interested in every detail of your life. He has resources and is able to help you succeed. Even we, who are confident in our own abilities, education, and resources to get things done, wisely trust Him. The advice from Scripture is simple, "Don't count on your war-horse to give you victory – for all of its strength, it cannot save you" (Psalm 33:17).

You may be limited, but He is limitless. He knows people and places and has vast resources and will favor you as you go along.

Joseph was a dreamer and his brothers hated him for it. The Bible tells us that they kidnapped him and sold him to a caravan of traveling business people heading to Egypt. They, in turn, sold Joseph to a man named Potiphar, an official to the pharaoh. Eventually Joseph found himself sitting in an Egyptian jail. Seventeen-year-old Joseph was far from home in a foreign land. He didn't know the Egyptian language. He had nothing to his name. He had no cash. Joseph did not know anyone who could help him. There was no way out of jail. All Joseph had were his dreams and his God. But that was enough. We will look at Joseph's story in greater detail in the next chapter, but for now let us look at one verse in the book of Genesis that you need to always remember for your own sake, "But the LORD was with Joseph and showed him mercy, and He gave him favor in the sight of the keeper of the prison." (Genesis 39:21 NKJV)

PRAY: "Lord, please give me favor in the eyes of _____." You can fill in that blank with the name of your boss, teacher, interviewing official, judge, the person you are meeting with, or anyone you are dealing with. Rather than going at it alone, partner with the Lord and let Him pave the way before you.

Once you have set a goal and a date, and you are bathing the whole thing in prayer, *become intentional* about pursuing your goals. Think ahead so you can connect your week's agenda with reaching your goal.

Often on Sundays I will write down the things I have to do for the coming week. I include something to do about reaching my goals in that list. Then as things get done, I cross them out. This may seem way too simple but it works for me. I know how distracted I can get as the days of the week roll along. Time can so easily be spent on the unimportant and unexpected. Prioritize!

The only thing left in the pursuit of your goals is to get started! The heckler of facts may try to discourage you, but do not let it. Do something about it. Get moving! People who require all the details addressed before proceeding never get going. The wisest teacher to ever live said, "Don't worry about tomorrow. It will take care of itself. You have enough to worry about today" (Matthew 6:34 CEV).

Don't be so concerned about what you don't know or those details you don't have answers for. You have what you need today. Go with that.

Dream Bigger

Abraham is the father of our faith. He and his wife also birthed what we know today as the Jewish Nation. Abraham experienced many miracles, victories against enemies, answered prayers, and great blessings. But his amazing journey of faith started in the simplest of ways:

"The LORD had said to Abram, 'Leave your native country, your relatives, and your father's family, and go to the land that I will show you. I will make you into a great nation. I will bless you and make you famous, and you will be a blessing to others. I will bless those who bless you and curse those who treat you with contempt. All the families on earth will be blessed through you.' So Abram departed as the LORD had instructed. Abram was seventy-five years old when he left Haran" (Genesis 12:1–4).

The facts were that Abram lived far from the Promised Land in a place where the God of heaven was not worshipped. Another fact was that even though God promised to make Abram into a great nation, he and his wife Sarai had been unable to have kids. Consider one more fact: God told him that all the families on earth would be blessed through Abram even though Abram knew only his country of origin. Those were the facts, but Abram believed God and followed. He may not have had all the details for the journey ahead, but he didn't need them anyway because his Father in heaven had all the bases covered. God would take care of the details.

The Lord has GREAT BIG PLANS for your life just like He had for *His boy* Abram. It may also be that the facts of who you are, where you live, and whatever situation you are in seem to contradict whatever seeds of vision the Lord planted in your heart. Don't let the heckler of facts discourage you. By faith, keep moving toward reaching your God-given dreams and passion in spite of your ignorance about how it all is going to come to pass. Socrates wrote, "True knowledge exists in knowing that you know nothing."

I challenge you to commit the following Bible verse to memory; it's one of my favorites, "Trust the LORD with all your heart, and don't depend on your own understanding. Remember the LORD in all you do, and he will give you success" (Proverbs 3:5–6 NCV).

I like the title of the tenth chapter of Dr. David Jeremiah's book *The Coming Economic Armageddon*. It is called, *Keep Your Head in the Game and Your Hope in God*.[10] That is what the author of Proverbs 3:5–6 is challenging us to do, to keep our eyes on the target and our hope in God.

The church I pastor, Lake Washington Fellowship, is vibrant and exciting and creative and contemporary and reaching people for the Kingdom. But it was not always like that. It was very traditional and set in its ways, reaching few, and it had grown stale through the years. We followed the same approach to church every week. God had given me a dream and vision for the place, but the facts were what they were.

As the years rolled we reached new people and built a new building. Then one year, the head of the Florida Baptist Convention at the time, planted a seed in my heart that changed my life forever. He asked if I would be interested in going to a *Creative Church Conference* in a place called Glorietta, New Mexico. I told him that I had not even heard about it but would be willing to go if I had the resources. He not only paid my entrance fee but the following week sent me airplane tickets to fly west. I was so excited to go. My heart was open to God's voice. While there I caught a vision for doing church in a more relevant and exciting way. After an evening session where author and speaker Lee Strobel spoke, I went back to my room, knelt by my bed and with many tears told God I was committed to following a new direction in ministry. I promised Him that I wasn't going back to doing church as usual any more. My soul had been refreshed, my vision redrawn, and my passion restored!

I went back home and did exactly what they warn conference attendees not to do: I started making changes right away. Through God's leading I was ready to fine-tune the organization regardless of cost. I went out on a flimsy limb trying hard to reach the fruit.

I called a meeting with all my leadership, shared my God-given vision for our church, and started restructuring Sunday morning services along with the entire organization.

At the beginning of the process everyone was on board with me. But as time went by even some of my close church friends and leaders became hecklers in my crowd.

When folks ask me about my twenty-nine year tenure at the church, I usually tell them that through the years our church has experienced two major exoduses of people and one mutiny. But in and through those messes, the Lord has called many from our congregation into full time Christian vocation, and He has used us to spiritually heal and fire up believers who had been hurt and spiritually burned by Christians in other ministries. Some of the meanest people I have ever known have been followers of Christ. I also tell them that, often, first time guests at our services get saved.

Our congregation continues to make an impact in our location and abroad in our support of missionaries. Groups of us have also traveled to share God's love in jungles and remote mountainous places in Third World countries. The point is that we have not allowed hecklers to keep us from the positive future the Lord has for us.

If the heckler of facts is harassing you, silence it by dreaming and pressing the issue of reaching your dreams no matter what.

Maybe right now the heckler of facts is challenging you and creating doubt in your mind, "Yeah, yeah, easy for him to say." The heckler tries to discourage you: "He's not wearing your shoes. There's no way anything like that will ever happen to you. Nothing's going to change where you are."

That's the same thing people said about Disney's dream.

What's Your Take?

1. In God's eyes, each of us is a masterpiece. Think creatively and share what kind of masterpiece you are like and why. Are you like a poem, a blockbuster movie or best seller, a great contemporary building, a graceful dancer, a detailed painting?
2. Share a big dream you have. It can be anything, even if it seems impossible at the present.
3. Still thinking of your dream, what roadblocks are between you and reaching your dream?
4. Has God ever done anything for you that you thought would never happen? Please share.
5. What emotions do you think Joseph may have experienced during his rejection and incarceration? Fear? Doubts? Anger and eventually bitterness? Questioning God?
6. The wise man wrote, "where there is no vision, the people perish" (Proverbs 29:18 KJV). What reasons would you give for that happening? Possible answers could be: vision gives us a target to aim at and direct our lives toward; vision gives hope and hope gives us a reason to live, but without hope there's little life in us; vision gives us an exciting prospect of a future worth looking forward to; without it life would be a passionless, slow death.

5

Dream Giver and Heckler Catcher

If God be your partner, make your plans large.

D.L. Moody

My dad was born and raised in Puerto Rico. He married and settled down in a place called Rio Piedras (River of Stones) where my brother and I grew up. He had a great family and a good job managing a large warehouse for a well-known department store on the island. But his life was about to change in a hurry. One night Dad had a dream from his heavenly Dream Giver. It was a dream that repeated itself ten times over the span of a few weeks.

In the dream Dad saw himself traveling along a highway he had never been on before. Along the way he came upon a beautiful lake with a big church in front of it. There was a sidewalk all around the lake for people to walk, exercise, and enjoy the scenery. Dad wouldn't have thought much of that dream, but because it repeated itself over and over, he thought that maybe God was trying to tell him something.

Sometime later, Dad and Mom decided to take a trip to Orlando, Florida, to check out the area and see what life was like in the States.

54

They had been thinking of a possible move because the unemployment and crime rate in the island were so high. While in Orlando they called a realtor to show them what houses were like and the man drove them around to show them a few. Along the way, Dad's dream came to life! They were traveling on State Road 408 (East–West expressway) when Dad saw beautiful Lake Underhill with an Alliance Church sitting right in front of it. It was the exact scene that had been repeated in his dreams. Dad grabbed Mom's hand, pointed out the window, and whispered, "That's the church, lake, and sidewalk I've been seeing in my dreams! God must be in this right now."

Eventually the realtor turned into a housing subdivision. In the distance mom saw a house with a fence around the property and said to the realtor, "See that corner house up ahead? That's the kind of house I want so my dogs can run around the yard." He answered, "Isn't that something? That's the house I'm about to show you." In a matter of a few hours my parents had bought that house, enrolled me as a senior in Colonial High School, and got my brother enrolled at Valencia Community College.

When they returned home they called a meeting with us kids and *Abu* (our Grandma) and said, "We're moving to Florida!" A few short months later Dad resigned from his job of many years and sold the house, and we all left to start afresh and anew in Florida.

I'll never forget looking back through the airplane's window at the shores of my beloved Puerto Rico as they disappeared from sight. It was both a sad and an exciting time as we all wondered what was ahead for us in Orlando. It never occurred to me, then a teenager, that our Dream Giver was in the process of redirecting and redefining our lives.

Life in Florida was difficult to get used to. I did not speak English and understood very little. I was going into my senior year of high school without friends. Everything was so different. There were no people on the streets. No stray dogs around. My brother and I felt like we were living in a ghost town. And when we went out, everyone looked so *white*. We were facing a serious culture shock. But God was in the process of working something out in our lives.

Years ago I heard that God is always at work around us, and that if we want to get into something really amazing we must join the Lord in whatever He is doing.

My mom and dad had recognized God at work during their trip to Orlando and took a bold step of faith in following Him. They did not know what all was ahead for them or how difficult the transition of moving to Orlando was going to be, but they did not really care. All they wanted was to remain obedient and faithful to the Lord. That resulted in great blessings from Him.

It is when you find yourself right smack in the middle of God's will that life takes on an amazing new meaning. If you are there, God bless you!

I know, however, many frustrated believers who are not there. Life has not been easy, their dreams have faded, and there is nothing but disturbing hurt inside. But God can change that! He has a way getting ahold of hecklers and eliminating them.

Dream Catchers

Do you like dream catchers? I have seen them inside homes and hanging from a rearview mirror, a necklace, and even key chains. The American Indian tradition of the dream catchers is fascinating. The people of the tribe would tie strings around a frame and hang it near a sleeping child. According to the tale, the dream catcher will act as a net where bad dreams get caught and good dreams are allowed to pass through so the children can rest at ease.

I want you to think of God as not only a giver of dreams but also a catcher of hecklers. He is able to protect you by catching your frustrations created by hecklers. You may ask, "But what if I can't seem to shake off from my mind the frustrating events of my past?"

God's Holy Spirit wants to transform your mind and the way you think—even filter whatever roams in your mind. He wants to replace your thoughts with His (Romans 12:1–2).

Dan (not his real name) is an older man who gave his heart to Christ the first Sunday he worshipped at our church. We met a few times and he told me his story. He was a veteran of war and for as long as he could remember he had not had a good night's sleep since the war. Nightmares of past war activities assaulted him every night, waking him up in a cold sweat. With tears streaming down his eyes he told me of some horrible things he had done as he followed orders. He asked me if the Lord would ever forgive him. The heckler of guilt was harassing him.

I told him about the mercy and grace of our great God and how, when he had trusted Jesus Christ as his Savior, the blood of Jesus had covered all his sins (Ephesians 1:7). I spoke to Dan about the fact that God says that He will no longer remember our sins (Psalm 103:12). Whatever wrong Dan had done, God had forgotten all about it when Dan laid his life at the foot of the cross.

I urged Dan to not only accept God's complete forgiveness but to also forgive himself in Jesus's name. I shared with Dan the Bible verse that says that those who are in Christ are new creatures, the old has passed away and a new life has begun (2Corinthians 5:17). Before our meeting was over I prayed for him and asked the Lord to completely deliver Dan from those nightmares, beginning that very night. Then I challenged Dan to pray and read Scripture before he went to sleep that night and every night from then on.

A few days later Dan made a point to find me. With tears in his eyes he told me that since our meeting he had been sleeping all night without nightmares. He was so excited and grateful to God, not only for saving his soul, but also for allowing him to overcome the misery he was living with. The Dream Giver had also become a Heckler Catcher!

Stone Cold Heart

Joseph's dad loved him so much that he gave him a beautiful coat of many colors while his eleven other brothers wore gray and earth tones. He was also a dreamer and his brothers resented him for it. They sold him as a slave and he ended up in a jail in Egypt.

Resentment is one of those emotions that tend to grow wild inside our hearts when left unchecked. Then, as it festers, resentment can turn to bitter hate.

Please allow me to revisit the story of Joseph that we went through in the last chapter. What the brothers did was a cold-hearted betrayal of trust. Picture the heart-wrenching scene as Joseph pleaded with his brothers for mercy; with many tears he begged his own flesh and blood not to send him away but to no avail. The brothers had become calloused hecklers in Joseph's crowd. Overnight the dreamer had become a slave and then a prisoner.

Many years later Joseph became the pharaoh's right hand man, the second most powerful man in Egypt. Then the heavenly dream giver became the heckler catcher. The Lord caught up with Joseph's brothers and laid a serious guilt trip on them for what they had done to their brother.

"They said to one another, 'Surely we are being punished because of our brother. We saw how distressed he was when he pleaded with us for his life, but we would not listen; that's why this distress has come on us'" (Genesis 42:21).

The Hebrew word for *distressed* means to live a nightmare, to experience the agony of the soul. It has to do with misery, despair, and painful suffering. Then the word *pleaded* means to beg. Joseph had begged his loved ones not to sell him into slavery. He may have even crawled on his knees crying and pleading for mercy. But their hearts were stone cold. Can you imagine the horrible scene?

Have you ever been hurt by people you trusted? It cuts deep to your core! You never forget the pain hecklers cause, the salty taste of tears, and the hollow feeling in your gut.

Many pastors and their families have experienced that; I know, because I am one of them. But anyone from any walk of life can go through the pain of broken trust. However, the dream giver and heckler catcher can help bring your dreams back into focus.

Straight From the Heart of God

When the people of Israel were living in misery because of their oppressors, the prophet Jeremiah wrote them something you can benefit from. They were words full of optimism and promise, and even though they were written for the Israelites, you too could adopt them as your own and let them give you hope. This is good stuff coming straight from the heart of God for all of us going through difficult circumstances, "Some time ago, the LORD appeared to me and told me to say… 'I will always love you; that's why I've been so patient and kind. You are precious to me… Once again you will dance for joy and play your tambourines… Young women and young men, together with the elderly, will celebrate and dance, because I will comfort them and turn their sorrow into happiness. I will bless my people…

So don't lose hope. I, the LORD, have spoken'" (Jeremiah 31:3, 4, 13, 14, 17 CEV).

Please read that over again slowly. Let God's love and hope take root in your heart. Allow His Holy Spirit to secretly, miraculously, and quietly begin a radical transforming work in you. He's an expert at it.

I have known people who were physically and emotionally hurt by some ill-willed individual. Their feelings of resentment consumed them to the point that they developed physical problems because of them.

The writer of the book of Hebrews issued this stern warning to his readers: "Look after each other so that none of you fails to receive the grace of God. Watch out that no poisonous root of bitterness grows up to trouble you, corrupting many" (Hebrews 12:15).

I'm sure Joseph replayed the scene of his brothers' betrayal hundreds of times as he sat in a dark, musty Egyptian jail. It would have been easy for him to become discouraged and bitter and, eventually, mentally and physically ill. He could have drowned in a sea of hate. But the Bible tells us nothing of the sort.

Joseph was not hopeless or in despair or bitter. Neither can you find anywhere the cancer of vengeance eating him up inside. Believe me, I am not trying to glorify this young Bible character. He was as human as any of us. I am sure he experienced moments of sadness, anger, and maybe even questioning; we will have to ask him when we meet him in heaven. The Bible just does not tell us. What we do know is that Joseph was wise beyond his years and he knew that he could trust God in his difficulties and trials.

The following words from the prophet Isaiah were directed to the nation of Israel. But they can be applicable to you and me, to how the Lord feels about you as a person and to the kind of promises you can hang onto when you are beginning to listen to the hecklers in your life.

"'Do not be afraid, for I have ransomed you. I have called you by name; you are mine. When you go through deep waters, I will be with you. When you go through rivers of difficulty, you will not drown. When you walk through the fire of oppression, you will not be burned up; the flames will not consume you. For I am the Lord, your God, the Holy One of Israel, your Savior'" (Isaiah 43:1b–3a).

Through the years I have learned that people who allow their hecklers to get the best of them live hurting, miserable lives. Painful memories have become their worst enemy. Their minds punish and rob them of joy and peace while the person who caused the damage has moved on without giving it another thought.

As hard as this may sound, the best thing to do is to let God catch your pain and dispose of it. Express your frustration and desire for payback to God, then let God handle it. He is just. God is the ultimate avenger and heckler catcher. "If someone does wrong to you, do not pay him back by doing wrong to him… My friends, do not try to punish others when they wrong you, but wait for God to punish them with his anger. It is written: 'I will punish those who do wrong; I will repay them,' says the Lord" (Romans 12:17a, 19 NCV).

Let's review the facts:

- Joseph had big dreams
- Joseph became a slave
- He ended up far away from home
- He was in jail
- Joseph couldn't communicate well because he did not speak Egyptian
- He had no money
- He had no friends
- He had no influence of any kind

Favored!

But Joseph became determined to get out of jail. Thirteen years later, Joseph became a free man, powerful and rich, and God blessed him with a precious family of his own.

You may be reading this thinking, *Things like that happen to other people but never to me.*

I challenge you to hang on tight to the Dream Giver and Heckler Catcher. The Bible is clear on how Joseph went from having nothing to getting everything, "The Lord was with Joseph and he prospered" (Genesis 39:2 NIV). If you're a person of faith you know that the Lord is with you when others are not. When you go through the storm, He is your peace. When you walk through valley of the shadow of death, He is your light. When your world collapses, Jesus reaches down to pull you up. I can't really explain it but that's how faith works.

One more Bible verse that has the power to revolutionize how you think: "But while Joseph was there in the prison, the Lord was with him; he showed him kindness and granted him favor in the eyes of the prison warden" (Genesis 39: 20b–21 NIV).

Never forget that God is always with you! His eyes are constantly on you 24/7. The Bible tells us that God never dozes off or goes to sleep on you (Psalm 121). I have a time in the afternoons that I call my stupid hour when I get ridiculously sleepy. It does not matter what I am doing, when stupid hour hits I'm good for nothing unless I gulp down a Red Bull or a delicious iced coffee.

The good news is that God does not have stupid hours. He is always fresh and attentive and will never turn His face from you. Jesus put it this way, "And be sure of this: I am with you always, even to the end of the age" (Matthew 28:20b).

God loves you and wants to load you up with good things. He showed favor and kindness to Joseph thousands of years ago, and He wants to do the same for you. Jesus said, "So if you sinful people know how to give good gifts to your children, how much more will your heavenly Father give good gifts to those who ask him" (Matthew 7:11).

I'll give the world to my girls (the one I married and the ones born to her). They may ask for little but I want to go beyond what they ask. Jesus's point was that if sinful, earthly dads can be good to their children, how much more will your heavenly Father, who is holy and perfect and who loves you and me with all His heart, be willing to give to those who look to Him? God wants to bless those who love Him.

One thing we mistakenly do is focus on the wrong that happens to us rather than the right. The result of that way of thinking is discouragement. If truth were told, the good things we have going on usually far outweigh the bad things. Focus on the good!

The media has given God such a bad rap. He is often portrayed as a mean old man in the sky ready to swing his stick at those not conforming to His standards. But nothing could be farther from the truth. John used three words that describe the Lord best, "God is love!" (1John 4:8b)

What a simple, clear, accurate description of God! When you put your faith in Jesus Christ to save your soul, you receive grace and mercy from God. You can go to Him at any time for anything, fully knowing He wants to love and care for you. He is paying attention to your every need.

Next time hecklers of any kind start making noise in your life, remind yourself that you are a child of God and ask Him to bless you in a big way and fight the battle for you. Give your heckler's names up to God and let Him settle your score His way. Then look for the Lord's favor on your life. God will use others to bless your life in one way or another. But you have to pay attention. If you are not careful you may miss all that God is doing, not only for your benefit but also for His purposes.

Think about the time the sales person gave you an extra percentage off your purchase or gave you a coupon you did not have to make the price even cheaper. Favor! What about the time the guy behind the glass counter at the cafeteria gave you the biggest piece of pie? Favor! Or when it was raining like crazy and you found the closest parking spot to the door at the mall. Favor! Or the time when, in the privacy of her office, your professor decided to put a plus sign next to your test score. Favor!

Not long ago one of my daughters found $300 on the street as she was walking downtown. Lucky you say? Favor, says I. God favors His children.

I pray for favor often. You should too. Ask the Lord to give you or someone you love favor in the eyes of someone else as He did for Joseph. For example, you can pray, "Lord, will you give my wife favor in the eyes of her employer? God, help her not only do well but go farther than anyone else in that company." You can ask for God to give you and yours favor in the eyes of teachers, judges, realtors, co-workers, bankers, and anyone else you all come into contact with. Let's say that you have a meeting scheduled. Ask the Lord to favor you with wisdom before you get to the meeting, with green lights when you're running late for that meeting, and to favor you in the eyes of the people you're meeting with.

It's amazing the kinds of things God does for those He loves. The apostle Paul wrote, "No eye has seen, no ear has heard, and no mind has imagined what God has prepared for those who love him" (1Corinthians 2:9).

When you spend too much time paying attention to what's disturbing, disrupting, and even tormenting your mind you'll most likely become paralyzed. Refuse to do that.

It is in the difficult times that true faith must shine! Let God help you overcome the obstacles in your way.

I was watching a boxing match on television some time back. Both men's eyes were almost swollen shut from the blows each had taken during the fight. One of the fighters was bleeding profusely from both his nose and a cut over his left eye. It was the seventh round when suddenly the trainer in that young man's corner threw a white towel into the ring. In boxing that's the way of telling the referee that you've had enough and you're quitting the fight.

It's easy sometimes to feel so beaten up that we just want to throw in the towel and call it quits. DON'T! Relax! Take a deep breath.

My brother Hector always reminded me to never to give up and never surrender. Make that your motto for living and dreaming and silencing the hecklers in your life. Sometimes overcoming has simply to do with gathering your thoughts, refocusing, and readjusting your mind.

When I was attending seminary one of my stress reducing activities was playing full court basketball with other students. There was one guy in particular who, on the heat of the competition, would say words that sounded foreign. When he would miss a shot or mess up he would yell something like "Kranz" and other similar nonsense. So I asked him about it and he told me that he had invented curse words that have absolutely no meaning. He did it to relieve stress without the danger of sinning.

How do you handle difficulties? Many years ago I went to a store to purchase some jewelry for my darling wife. This store had an enormous jewelry counter that was packed with people wanting to find the perfect Christmas gift for their loved ones. But it was intense. There was no numbering system being followed. It was a first come first serve kind of thing but the employees behind the counter had no clue which customer was next. The scene reminded me of a bar full of demanding thirsty drinkers.

I tried to be polite but was getting nowhere. In fact people show-ing up after me were being served before me. I was frustrated! Finally, after 45 minutes of trying to get someone's attention behind the counter, I was helped. However, the employee told me that the item I wanted had been sold a few minutes earlier. I was steaming mad. I got back in my car, closed the windows, and drove away. Then I yelled as loud as I could. If you have ever done that you know how good it feels.

Maybe as you read this you feel like the negatives are stacked high against you. One bad thing has been following another and all that is left in you is a resentful, angry disposition. Do not let those feelings eat you up inside. Life can turn around in moments.

In the story of Joseph, after the Egyptian pharaoh had a bother-some dream he could not figure out, Joseph was pulled out of jail and given the chance to interpret it. And when he did God blessed him immensely.

"Joseph's suggestions were well received by Pharaoh and his offi-cials. So Pharaoh asked his officials, 'Can we find anyone else like this man so obviously filled with the spirit of God?' Then Pharaoh said to Joseph, 'Since God has revealed the meaning of the dreams to you, clearly no one else is as intelligent or wise as you are. You will be in charge of my court, and all my people will take orders from you. Only I, sitting on my throne, will have a rank higher than yours.'

"Pharaoh said to Joseph, 'I hereby put you in charge of the entire land of Egypt.' Then Pharaoh removed his signet ring from his hand and placed it on Joseph's finger. He dressed him in fine linen cloth-ing and hung a gold chain around his neck. Then he had Joseph ride in the chariot reserved for his second-in-command. And wherever Joseph went, the command was shouted, "Kneel down!" So Pharaoh put Joseph in charge of all Egypt. And Pharaoh said to him, 'I am Pharaoh, but no one will lift a hand or foot in the entire land of Egypt without your approval.'

"Then Pharaoh gave Joseph a new Egyptian name, Zaphenath-paneah. He also gave him a wife, whose name was Asenath. She was the daughter of Potiphera, the priest of On. So Joseph took charge of the entire land of Egypt" (Genesis 41:37–45).

What if Joseph had given up on his dreams and become resentful while sitting in jail? He may have never experienced the greatness the dream giver and heckler catcher wanted to give him. Joseph's unjust incarceration seemingly stole thirteen precious years of Joseph's life, but in the end, God raised him up to live like a king.

The question is how did Joseph not give in to resentment? How was he able to silence the heckler of resentment? One word: Perspective!

Perspective is being able to see beyond the way things appear. In Joseph's case it would appear as if the abandonment of his brothers was followed by the abandonment of God. However, he was able to discern that there was a higher plan going on.

Later, after he and his brothers (his betrayers) were reunited, Joseph said to them, "You intended to harm me, but God intended it all for good. He brought me to this position so I could save the lives of many people" (Genesis 50:20).

Ask the Lord to give you an angle to your situation that you have not seen before. The Holy Spirit will help you look beyond to the prospect of something better coming your way.

A Domino Effect

When my dad moved to North America because of his recurring dream, he faced nothing but difficulties and no job. People even made fun of Dad's rough English. Eventually Dad settled for buying a coin laundry. Mom and Dad worked that business six days a week from early in the morning to nighttime just to make ends meet. It almost sucked the life out of them. Dad could have given in to the heckler of frustration, thrown his hands in the air, and said, "I give up. What's the use?" But the opposite happened! He and Mom gave themselves more than ever before to the Lord. As a result a great spiritual domino effect happened:

- Mom and Dad became fully surrendered to Jesus as Savior
- Dad became a deacon of a church and eventually earned an Associate's of Ministry Degree
- Dad became a pastor of a Spanish mission in Orlando, Florida
- Dad's three sisters were saved through his story/testimony
- Dad's nephew gave his heart to Christ for the same reason
- Some of Dad's co-workers at a department store became believers
- My brother was born again
- His wife was born again
- My brother's children turned their lives over to the Lord
- I was born again
- The girl I married, the love of my life, was saved
- My two daughters surrendered to Jesus
- My wife's mother became a Christian
- My wife's father became active in church again
- My wife's brother told me he had made his peace with God
- My wife's sister and daughter turned to the Lord
- My wife's brother-in-law trusted Jesus as Savior and surrendered his life to serving the Lord in church ministry
- I sensed God calling me to surrender my life to ministry and to pastor a church
- My wife surrendered to full time ministry work (as my biggest encourager)

- I've had the privilege of leading many to Christ through the Holy Spirit's work in my life, as a witness and a preacher
- Many people's lives have been helped and ministered to and changed through God's work in the church I pastor
- The list can go on. God has worked in incredible ways, and it all started with a dream. I'm sure if you sat down and thought about it, you too could put a list together of the blessings of God in your life.

I close this chapter with this story: When I first arrived at Lake Washington Fellowship, a godly woman by the name of Nellie asked me to join her in a walk around the property. When we got to the front of the church she pointed to the large grassy field in front of the church building and said, "You see that land, preacher? Our dream is to grow and build a new church right there. We need to pray and reach people."

The fascinating thing is that before accepting the church's offer to become their pastor I had been warned by someone on the outside not to become the pastor of this church. I was told that it was a place that was really rough on pastors. And in all truth the congregation did have a rich history of turbulence. But Nellie had held on to the dream!

As my family and I began to minister here we faced the fury of hecklers at various times. It was painful and difficult. But we let God be our dream giver and heckler catcher. We had to ride over some seriously painful problems, but the Lord came through for us time and again. Today the church is better than it has ever been, and a very nice building now sits where Nellie once dreamed.

What's Your Take?

1. This chapter begins with the story of the author's dad having a dream that came true. Can you describe a dream you had that came true?

2. Reread out loud the words the prophet Jeremiah wrote for the people of God when they were going through rough times: "Some time ago, the LORD appeared to me and told me to say... 'I will always love you... You are precious to me... Once again you will dance for joy and play your tambourines... Young women and young men, together with the elderly, will celebrate and dance, because I will comfort them and turn their sorrow into happiness. I will bless my people... So don't lose hope. I, the LORD, have spoken" (Jeremiah 31:3, 4, 13, 14, 17 CEV). What comes to your mind when you think of that kind of celebration? How do these verses contrast the false idea that God is like a mean old man relishing in the suffering of people here on earth?

3. Jesus compared the heavenly Father to a loving father who will go above and beyond to give good gifts to people. Do you have a memory of your dad or a father figure who was very loving and good to you?

4. God loves to favor His own! Share an experience when you felt you received favor from God and ask others to do the same.

5. The Lord will fight for us when hecklers do us wrong. He is the original avenger! The Old Testament character David had a different thought about dealing with his troublemakers. Read the following verses: "Break the arms of these wicked, evil people! Go after them until the last one is destroyed" (Psalm 10:15); "Break the teeth in their mouths, O

God; Lord, tear out the fangs of those lions!" (Psalm 58:6 NIV); "Let their supper be bait in a trap that snaps shut; May their best friends be trappers who'll skin them alive" (Psalm 69:22 MSG); "Let death stalk my enemies; let the grave swallow them alive, for evil makes its home within them" (Psalm 55:15); and, "But I say, love your enemies! Pray for those who persecute you!" (Matthew 5:44) At this time please ask the following question: If you were given a choice, which of those would you pick for your enemies? Which is easier, to wish for bad to happen to others or let God do the fighting for you? Is what Jesus is saying possible to do?

6. At the end of the chapter, the author described a spiritual domino effect because of faithfulness. Can you think of a time when you experienced God's domino effect?

PART 3

Defending Your Home Turf

6

The Heckler Within

If you hear a voice within you say *you
cannot paint,* then by all means paint
and that voice will be silenced.

Vincent van Gogh

Logic is how we operate. God pre-wired us that way; the ability to
think rationally and figure things out separates us from hairy mon-
keys. The voice of reason helps us come to conclusions. After pon-
dering the pros and cons and talking to others about a given matter,
we make prudent decisions. Reasoning is about intellect, intuition,
learning, and intelligence. Psychologists call it the cognitive process.
Sometimes we refer to it as *the small voice within.*

However, when you are a Christian, another still, small voice is
within you, the Holy Spirit's. These two voices will sometimes speak
simultaneously, leading you in two opposite directions: your logical
voice sometimes leading to do evil and the Spirit's voice leading to do
what is right in God's eyes. At that time you must choose the latter
and forsake the former.

In the book *Recapture the Wonder* by Ravi Zacharias there's an
amazing story about a woman who became pregnant with an un-
wanted baby. She was angry and decided to have an abortion. After

she was prepped for the procedure the doctor came in and was about to inject her with something when a nurse came into the room and told the doctor of an emergency phone call that needed his attention.

When the doctor stepped out of the room the woman's attention was drawn to the sonogram monitor. She saw the image of the baby in her womb and recognized the seriousness of the situation. She then quickly got dressed and left the clinic. She carried the baby full term and today the almost aborted baby is a beautiful young woman and the love of her mother's heart. When talking about the courage it took to do the right thing by leaving the doctor's office that day she doesn't take the credit for it but says it was the voice of God in her telling her what to do.[11]

God always leads you in the right direction. Trust Him!

The two small voices within you will also have conflicting messages about pursuing your God-given dreams and those great things you set your heart to do. One voice, the heckler within you, will claim that big things happen to others but not to you. It will counsel you to abandon your dreams and settle for what you already have. That kind of thinking may come from your past failures and experiences and a damaged sense of worth. The other voice, the Holy Spirit within you, will drive you to trust God and push forward!

This is a critical juncture when you have to defend your home turf, the person God created you to be. When the heckler within tries to devalue you, revert in your mind to the Truth that you were fearfully and wonderfully made and that you belong to God!

Remember that the GREAT BIG GOD in Heaven loves you most. He wants to restore you and give you a future. That is what God did for David, the shepherd boy-turned king. He wrote Psalm 40. The first three verses of that passage tell us the kinds of things God can do: "I waited patiently for the LORD to help me, and he turned to me and heard my cry. He lifted me out of the pit of despair, out of the mud and the mire. He set my feet on solid ground and steadied me as I walked along. He has given me a new song to sing, a hymn of praise to our God." (Psalm 40:1–3a).

No one really knows why the greatest king of Israel wrote those words, but it probably had something to do with the days before David was crowned. One day while David was still a young shepherd, a prophet of God anointed him to be king of Israel. The ceremony was short and private. Only David's family was present.

For a while nothing changed for him, but then doors of opportunity began to open. David got his foot in the door of politics with a job serving King Saul in the palace. He also found fame in Israel by killing Goliath, the giant. But King Saul became insanely jealous of David and tried to kill him. So he became a fugitive! For the next several years David lived on the run. Fulfilling his purpose and dream of being king must have seemed so far away.

His inner heckler may have made David think that he would never be king. His mind could have played dirty tricks on him, telling him that he would always be a shepherd and that the little anointing ceremony at his house never really did happen. Beyond that, the facts were stacked against David; he was Israel's most wanted and a man without a country. Unless something radical happened, there was no way David would ever become king. All those reasons may have contributed to David being in despair and needing help from the Lord.

Your mind will play tricks on you, too, making you think you will not live up to your true potential. Don't believe it.

David patiently waited and cried out to God. Then the Lord lifted David's spirit, set him on the road to success, and put a song in his heart. In other words, the heckler within was silenced by the still, small voice of God.

For our lives, especially in this fast-paced twenty-first century, the key is to pay attention so we do not miss that whispering voice of

God. We live in a world that is full of noise. Society has set attention grabbers everywhere we turn. When we're not careful, we can easily miss whatever work the Lord may be trying to do within us.

Elijah was a prophet in tennis shoes. He was Israel's most wanted and was on the run from wicked Queen Jezebel. She had vowed to kill him by all possible means. So the prophet was afraid and hiding. His heckling voice within told him he was nothing more than a dead man walking. Elijah even asked God to kill him and put him out of his misery—a prayer the Lord did not answer. The man was under a lot of stress.

Then one day while Elijah was hiding in a cave, God spoke to him: "The LORD said, "Go out and stand on the mountain in the presence of the LORD, for the LORD is about to pass by." Then a great and powerful wind tore the mountains apart and shattered the rocks before the LORD, but the LORD was not in the wind. After the wind there was an earthquake, but the LORD was not in the earthquake. After the earthquake came a fire, but the LORD was not in the fire. And after the fire came a gentle whisper. When Elijah heard it, he pulled his cloak over his face and went out and stood at the mouth of the cave. Then a voice said to him, "What are you doing here, Elijah?'" (1Kings 19:11–13 NIV)

When you read the rest of the story, you find that the Lord gave Elijah instructions on where to go and what to do next. The point is that God communicated through a gentle whisper and not the fantastic events that preceded it.

Sometimes people look for God to speak to them through great and wonderful things or through supernatural miraculous events. You may be looking for clear-cut directions for your life, and you may find them, but make sure you do not miss God in the small things. Most often His leading comes through nothing more than a Bible verse and a sense of peace in your prayer life. Regardless, pay attention to His voice and follow Him.

If Indiana Jones Can Do It, So Can I

I challenge you to listen to God's Spirit rather than your heckler within.

Faith has been defined as confidence, hope, and being certain of a future you can't still lay a hold of (Hebrews 11:1).

People who live by faith know in their heart that what they are thinking about and dreaming of is theirs for the taking. The intangible, invisible faith, to them, is as real as things they can see with their eyes and touch with their fingers. They make decisions and take steps of faith, certain that God is not going to let them fall.

In the third *Indiana Jones* movie, the adventurous explorer Dr. Jones comes to a point in his journey where taking a resolute and seemingly dangerous step of faith is required. The life of his father depends on it! Indiana's physical journey of finding the Holy Grail that would bring healing to his dad becomes a soul-searching journey of faith. Indiana gets to the edge of a rocky cliff and must reach the other side even when it looks like an impossible feat.

In a climactic moment in the movie, the whispering voice of reason holding Indiana Jones back gives way to the voice of faith inside him telling him to keep going, to take a step purely based on faith. Indiana is frightened. He grabs his chest as if holding back his pounding heart and with nothing but a prayer takes a forward step into the abyss. Moviegoers are on the edge of their seats in a crescendo of emotion only to breathe a sigh of relief as Dr. Jones's foot hits solid ground underneath. Only after taking that first step does the explorer realize that there is a rocky trail there, invisible to the naked eye, as it had blended with the rocky cliff scenery before him.

By the way, there's potential in everything. Take marriage, for example: Regardless of the state it is in today, your marriage has the possibility of being the best relationship on the planet. Think of your talents, giftedness, and personality; any one of those or a combination of them has the potential to send you soaring. Schooling and past experiences can also open doors that can take you far beyond what you've known.

The Age-Defying You

As I get older, that heckler's voice in me is becoming louder and louder, *Jorge Acevedo, you've reached your ceiling. Your career won't go much farther.* That demon on my shoulder tells me that I should be satisfied with what I have, that I'm not getting any younger, that I will never reach my dreams, and that soon I will start going downhill. Depressing!

When I turned forty I hit the *wall of doom*. It was the dreaded midlife crisis. My vision blurred. I needed glasses. My belly plummeted, adding inches to my pant size. My *chichos* (Spanish for love handles) protruded beyond the waistline of my snugly fitted jeans and became easy to grab. I was suffering from MTS (Muffin Top Syndrome). Those were difficult days for sure!

Overcoming the midlife crisis required me to make a conscious choice to pay attention to God's whispering voice within telling me that the best is yet to come.

Today I'm more excited than ever about what the future holds. I'm buying into the idea that the forties and fifties are the new twenties and thirties (or something like that). I'm feeling young and energized, anticipating new opportunities to come my way. Maybe you are in the same stage of life. Wonderful! Buckle up and hang right in there. The ride is about to get good.

The Atlantis Paradise Island Resort in Nassau, Bahamas, is an amazing place of stunning décor and meticulously kept landscape. You can spend hours soaking up the sun, exploring all kinds of sea life in the aquariums, or riding delightful water slides.

I was there with my family a few years ago. I was walking around looking for my daughters, nieces, and nephews and found them at the top of something called the Power Tower. They were ready to go on a scary two-hundred-foot-long, insanely dark body slide that has a fifty-foot near-vertical drop called the Abyss.

My adrenalin was rushing as they all urged me to go down the terrifying water hole. The caution instructions tell the would-be rider that people with fear of heights, high speeds, darkness, and enclosed places should avoid going down it. And that people with heart problems should not ride it. I don't have heart problems but felt like I was developing one at that moment.

As I looked at the narrow opening of rushing water beneath me I said: "A man my age shouldn't be doing things like this." But I jumped in and screamed like a schoolgirl until I plunged into a pool of water in a subterranean lagoon. I'm not sure if I'll ever try that fourteen-second thrill ride again, but the Abyss reminded me of my life stage: *Cautious, why risk it?* That may not be an inherently bad trait to live by, but it certainly does not apply to following God's spiritual lead in your life.

The Lazy Man River was another water ride around the park. That one seemed more my speed. My darling wife and I got into a two-person floating doughnut and did some chilling on it. That is, until we hit the wave machine that turns the lazy man experience into crazy fast rapids. There was no escaping it either. We tried paddling against the stream with our arms to no avail. We were in there for keeps. As we picked up speed we tumbled, turned, and got knocked against the rocks a few times, but we finished strong. The fascinating thing is that when the ride was over we wanted more of it, so we stayed in for a second round of action!

Your heckler within will yell at you, *SLOW DOWN* and coast through the stream of your life's accomplishments. I say, "Forget that jazz!" Regardless of your age, fun rapids may still lie ahead! Get ready to ride whatever wave lies before you! What if the best is yet to come? I am reminded of a Bible character named Caleb who did not know the meaning of the word quit:

"A delegation from the tribe of Judah, led by Caleb son of Jephunneh the Kenizzite, came to Joshua at Gilgal. Caleb said to Joshua, "Remember what the LORD said to Moses, the man of God, about you and me when we were at Kadesh-barnea. I was forty years old when Moses, the servant of the LORD, sent me from Kadesh-barnea to explore the land of Canaan. I returned and gave an honest report, but my brothers who went with me frightened the people from entering the Promised Land. For my part, I wholeheartedly followed the LORD my God. So that day Moses solemnly promised me, 'The land of Canaan on which you were just walking will be your grant of land and that of your descendants forever, because you wholeheartedly followed the LORD my God.'

"Now, as you can see, the LORD has kept me alive and well as he promised for all these forty-five years since Moses made this promise—even while Israel wandered in the wilderness. Today I am eighty-five years old. I am as strong now as I was when Moses sent me on that journey, and I can still travel and fight as well as I could then. So give me the hill country that the LORD promised me. You will remember that as scouts we found the descendants of Anak living there in great, walled towns. But if the LORD is with me, I will drive them out of the land, just as the LORD said" (Joshua 14:6–12).

Eighty-five-year-old Caleb silenced his heckler within with conviction! He took the land God had promised him forty years earlier.

Caleb would not be denied! He refused to let age be a factor in his forward push. At eighty-five he was ready for a fight. And eventually he conquered the land and zoned it, and he and his people enjoyed it!

The key to such incredibly rewarding blessing from God is that Caleb had lived by conviction and faith. He believed that the same Lord who had made the promise would deliver it.

How about you? How much do you seriously believe that this God of Heaven whom you can't hear, see, or touch can be trusted to make good on His promises?

I am challenging you to listen to the quiet voice of God inside you urging you to keep moving ahead. Sometimes what God wants may contradict what you know and have always done, but that's when faith must take over.

It Happened at Walmart

My friend Ray is the drummer in our church band. Something great and faith related happened to him recently. He gave me permission to share his story:

One Sunday morning I was leaving church and went to a superstore in town. I saw a woman in her mid to late thirties in a red hoody. As I looked her way she sneaked something into her hoody. She looked at me in shock and said: "I have two small children starving at home and I don't know what else to do." When she said that, I wanted to help her but I did not know what to do. I had no cash but I had my credit and debit card. So I thought if I bought something I could get cash back to give to her. So when I told her, "I will be right back," she said, "Why do you have to turn me in? Don't you know I have children that

are starving at home and I am just trying to feed my children?"
I said, "I am not trying to turn you in." I did not know how to
reassure her.

Our church has been reading *Draw The Circle: The 40 Day
Prayer Challenge* by Mark Batterson. This book says to never be
ashamed or embarrassed to pray in front of others. So I asked
her to pray with me but she said, "I have been praying, I have
prayed, and nothing happens. What good is it? I need food, not
prayer." So I wanted to reassure I was not going to turn her in so
I said, "Please pray with me." She again said, "What good is it?
It won't do anything for me. I'm tired of praying." So I reached
out my hands and asked her, "What do you have to lose? Please
pray with me."

She grabbed my hand and I thought to myself, *What am I
going to do? What am I going to say?* So I thought of my pastor,
Jorge Acevedo, and thought, *What would he say?* So I closed my
eyes and said, "Please help me, Lord. Help me help this woman. Help her the way you helped me in the past. Help her with
her children, food, and anything else. She has two kids at home
starving that need food and this woman needs help."

As I was praying with her I felt a hand on my left shoulder
for a split second. I said to myself, *Is this God? Is this an angel?* I
didn't want to open my eyes but I said to myself, *Let this happen,
please.* When I opened my eyes a woman was standing next to
us. She said she worked for an organization called Angel Harvest
and that she was going to help her with food.

At that moment I picked up M&Ms so I could buy them to
get cash back. I took out $40 and went back to where the two
women were. I reached out to hand her the $40 and she said,
"No, thank you. This lady is going to help me with food." I told

her to still take it in case she had other expenses. When I gave her the money she started crying and hugged me. I got choked up and almost started crying, too, because I was happy how things turned out.

When I left church I was in a good mood like always, and after the incident at Walmart, a feeling came over me of peace and happiness. Before, if I had seen her stealing, I would have turned my face and let it happen. Now, however, I felt it was my Christian duty to help.

The quiet Spirit of the Living God will sometimes lead you in an opposite way to what you are used to. And at first you may want to resist Him. Don't. It's the only way to silence the heckler within.

Do your eyes of understanding show you something that threatens what God is leading you to? It may not be age trying to slow you down; it may be gender or culture or language of origin or a criminal record or a credit score or a physical handicap or something else. Who is telling you that your dreams are too big to pursue and too hard to accomplish? After a while that negative voice sounds as annoying as the adults in the Peanuts cartoons: "Waa, waa, waa, waa, waa, waa."

To silence that heckler you must be confident and determined to do exactly what the negative voice within says you can't do. Years ago I heard Zig Ziglar say that confidence is like going after Moby Dick in a rowboat and taking the tartar sauce with you.

Two voices within you: One tells you to play it safe. The other, the still, small voice of God, tells you that all things are possible to people who believe Him. Unlocking your full potential comes only through silencing the former and listening to the latter. Which are you going to listen to?

Let's Go to the Jungle

Years ago while living in Florida, a couple of missionary friends felt the voice of God telling them to leave everything they knew—family, friends, and the comforts of life in the USA—and move to a dense jungle to reach out to complete strangers and minister to them in the name of Jesus. Years later they invited me to preach a conference for the indigenous people of that area. Three close friends joined my oldest daughter, Amanda, and I for the journey to this extremely remote area.

We flew into the city of Cochabamba, Bolivia, and from there boarded a small plane. It flew us over the peaks of steep high mountains before quickly dropping altitude to get us to the jungle below. The pain in our ears was almost unbearable, but we made it and landed on a short grassy strip between the waters of a winding Chapare River.

During the next several days we lived with my friends and their children in what seemed like the middle of nowhere. Nights were dark, days were extremely hot and humid, and when it rained, it rained intensely. We met many people and visited some of their simple communities. We traveled in canoes made of hollowed-out trees. From a distance we saw killer bees, while up close we watched army ants at work. We looked into a tarantula's nest on a jungle trail and paid a native woman to wash our clothes by the river's edge. She beat the garbage out of them with a stick. Among other things, we ate *jochi,* the world's biggest rat. It was delicious!

Our trip was memorable and definitely a once-in-a-lifetime event. But our missionary friends planned to stay there as long as God wanted them there. They had given their lives to reaching the people in that part of the world.

You may be saying to yourself, *I could never do that.* Or you may be wondering what would motivate someone to move to a place like that. The answer is simple: God! Faith in Him was the determining factor for our friends to pack up their bags and raise a family in a jungle. The apostle Paul wrote, "God is working in you to help you want to do and be able to do what pleases him" (Philippians 2:13b NCV).

The truth is that the Lord will not lead you to a place where He cannot keep you. He will be faithful to you and be the wind beneath your wings!

While on vacation by the Gulf of Mexico, I saw something in the water I had never seen before. A Jet Ski had something like a 25-foot fire hose connected to one of its exhausts. The other end of the fire hose was connected to the bottom of a wide, short board resembling a surfboard. The airflow pressure from the slow-moving Jet Ski propelled the short-board rider so he/she could wakeboard. Then at times the wake boarder would rise over the water and for several seconds it looked as if the person was surfing the wind. It looked amazing!

View God as the One who shoots you forward with purpose. He not only pushes you but also holds you and provides for you. His voice will challenge logic, disturb reasoning, and quiet the heckling voice within you that is trying to hold you back. Trust Him! Obey Him. Follow Him and get ready for the ride of a lifetime with an amazing, breathtaking view.

What's Your Take?

1. How would you describe the whispering voice of the Holy Spirit in your heart?
2. What voices do you think compete with the voice of God in your heart? How important to you is finding times of silence during your day? Do you have a specific place that you like visit to find peace and quiet?

3. The author described Indiana Jones having to take a step of faith that at the time seemed impossible. Have you ever wrestled with doing something that you felt the Lord was leading you to that required lots of faith?

4. Give a brief definition of faith.

5. Pastor Jorge described some friends who left everything to live in a South American jungle to try to win people to Jesus. Can you remember a time when you felt the Lord telling you to step out of your comfort zone to do something for Him?

6. God calls some Christians to be missionaries and some to work in a full time Christian vocation, but He calls everyone to love others and minister to them in His name. Think of some things you could do in Jesus's name on a regular basis that will make an impact in the Kingdom of God.

7. How would you know it is His whispering voice you hear? What would be the danger of allowing positive or negative circumstances and events to become the determining factor in what you think you ought to do?

7

Heckler Interrupted: And His Beat Goes On

Live life as if there's a party going on inside you!

LET'S TAKE A break from the obnoxious hecklers in our lives so we can focus on what drives you, what motivates you, what you love to do.

I love music. Many years ago when my wife and I lived in New Orleans, we visited Preservation Hall. Some of the best jazz musicians in New Orleans have played there. The place was so packed we had to sit on the floor next to an older *cat* playing the bass guitar. The musicians were jamming; my head was bobbing and my foot tapping. My Latino rhythm had taken over. It was magical! At the end of one of those songs the bass player leaned over to talk to me. For a moment I thought he was going to say something like, "Yeah, that's what I'm talking about." Instead, with a tone of reproach he said, "Hey, stop doing that!" A little defensively I asked, "Stop doing what?" He replied, "Stop tapping your foot on my chair. You're off beat and you're throwing me off rhythm, man." So much for magic…but I do love good music and rhythm.

Everyone has some sort of music running through their soul as they do what they love.

I'll never forget a police officer I saw directing traffic at an intersection. The traffic light was out and he was signaling cars to stop and go to keep the flow of traffic. But he was doing it with style and movements. Once he mimed as if pulling the car of a hesitating driver to move forward. Other times he would make a 180-degree turn like Michael Jackson and point a driver in a certain direction. Or he would put one hand behind his ear as if trying to listen to the drivers and pop some moves of his own. It was very entertaining. That cop was moving at the rhythm of his own beat.

Some love to dance! Others enjoy making people smile and laugh. I have friends with a wide variety of passions: Jim loves sci-fi and superheroes; Joe loves to learn and try out new activities; Mike loves to sell; John and Brian love working on cars. I know people who are passionate about animals. What do you love to do?

Truett Cathy, founder of Chick-fil-A, was passionate about the chicken sandwich. Walt Disney was passionate about dreaming and making others' dreams come true. My Spanish literature professor in college was passionate about Cervantes. My friend Tom is passionate about his Florida Gators. His twin brother, Gene, loves his Mets. And my friend Ryan so loves his Chicago Cubs that he flew there to watch them play in the World Series, the one they eventually won!

Let's define the word 'passion' as an intense emotional energy put into motion.

My friend Bill (not his real name) had dual passions: eyes and painting. After he retired from a successful career as an optometrist, Bill developed a love for painting. One of his oils hangs on my living room wall. What's your passion? Writing? Teaching? Building something? Planting and harvesting? Influencing others? Sports?

Let's do a quick exercise. Please STOP READING and mark this page. Find a pen and a blank piece of paper. Now jot down two things you love to do that you are passionate about. When you're done, put your pen down, find this exact spot, and keep reading. We will get to those two ideas you wrote down later. Thank you.

Do you know anyone who's passionate about God? I do not mean a person who is showy with an exaggerated portrayal of religious observances. I mean someone who genuinely loves Jesus Christ. It shows in their actions. There is a spiritual beat going on inside them and they are swaying with it. It is the beat of their Heavenly Drummer. Do you know anyone like that?

When I was starting college, I was a member of First Baptist Church in Orlando, Florida. Dr. Jim Henry was the pastor of that great church. One of his thousands of members was Mary (not her real name), an unusual young lady younger than me. She battled cancer, which eventually took her life.

I remember a couple of things about her. One, she loved anything Snoopy. Two, she loved Jesus with all her heart! That is what made her so unusual. As a young Christian, I had never met anyone who lived with such hope while in the face of such adversity. Her presence lit up a room. Her smile was contagious. When Mary went to heaven, the church auditorium was packed with over a thousand people in honor of that teenager. What made Mary special is that she was swaying to the beat of her Savior.

Jesus said, "The thief's purpose is to kill, steal and destroy. My purpose is to give them a rich and satisfying life" (John 10:10).

Notice that this overflowing life, which the Lord has in mind for all who believe, is not dependent on the circumstances around us but on Jesus Himself. He wants to be your satisfaction, the song in your heart, and the spring in your step! Mary was going through difficult, painful times, but the Holy Spirit within her gave her deep peace and joy.

One Crazy Beat

Let's return to the scene of David and Goliath that we briefly discussed in chapter three. No one but David was willing to fight Goliath.

If legendary boxing announcer Michael Buffer had introduced the bout, he might have said something like this: "Let's get ready to rummmmmmmble! In the Israeli corner, wearing old shepherd's clothes and armed with a handy dandy slingshot, is the challenger, Daaaaavid. In the Philistine corner, wearing a shiny full suit of armor and armed with a spear, is the undisputed heavyweight champion of the worrrrrllllllllld, Goliath."

It was an obvious mismatch. But David's passion for the Lord overruled any mental possibility of failure against his formidable opponent. While everyone else was thinking *Goliath is too big to hit,* David was thinking *he's too big to miss.*

So when David heard Goliath trash-talking the God of the Israeli army, he took on the rascal. Spunky guy, that David! He was swaying to the crazy beat of his Heavenly Drummer.

David stepped into the match with nothing but his slingshot and five smooth stones. Then he yelled at Goliath, "Everybody here will see that the Lord doesn't need swords or spears to save his people. The Lord always wins his battles, and he will help us defeat you" (1Samuel 17:47 CEV).

What happened next, as they say, is in the books. David launched a stone from his slingshot that accurately hit Goliath's head at the one place not protected by his bronze helmet, and Goliath was out cold! David had gained the victory!

The point is that David was swaying to the music being played by God's Spirit within him. Of course you know that I'm not referring to musical notes or a certain tune but to the leading of the Holy Spirit. He, God's Spirit, was the One who helped David believe he could overcome ridicule, lack of military training, youthfulness, and whatever else stood in his way.

God gives His people an advantage that catapults them to success.

Bandages and Stitches

There will be negative people, obstacles, difficult circumstances, problems, evil schemes against you (and the people you love), and a whole bunch of other things that will have a negative impact in your life. So many situations have the potential of throwing you off beat and turning your passion to the off position. I've been there. It's an awful feeling.

That is why falling in love with the Lord Jesus is essential to living a full and exciting life! He has the ability to heal your open emotional wounds, clean up whatever is harmful and hurtful, restore your broken spirit, sew you back up, and help you get back on your feet so you can move forward. "The Lord hears his people when they call to him for help. He rescues them from all their troubles. The Lord is close to the brokenhearted; he rescues those whose spirits are crushed. The righteous person faces many troubles, but the Lord comes to the rescue each time" (Psalm 34:17–19). The word '*brokenhearted*' in this passage means broken in many pieces.

I can't help think back to what happened to Humpty Dumpty. He was sitting on a wall seemingly having a great time. That is what wall-sitting is all about—taking it easy or chilling with friends or admiring the view or meditating. All of a sudden Humpty fell and broke into many pieces. The proverbial question in our minds has always been, *who pushed him?* No one will ever know.

I know this is a silly illustration but, just for the fun of it, can you imagine the nasty mess Humpty made at the bottom of that wall?

Shell, yolk, white, dirt, pebbles, and loose grass all mixed together. No wonder all the king's men couldn't help poor Dumpy. This was a job, let's imagine, that only the king himself could do!

You may feel like your life has been broken beyond repair. You feel miserable and without hope. But the King of Kings is able to help! One truth of Scripture is that the Lord is never beyond reach. He is always near! "He heals the brokenhearted and bandages their wounds" (Psalm 147:3).

When I was eleven years old, my brother, Hector, and I were delivering newspapers around some neighborhoods in the island. I rode on the back of his motorcycle while he drove. We were just a few blocks away from turning onto the street where we lived when a lady ran a stop sign and T-boned my brother's bike. Eyewitnesses claimed I flew at least twenty feet into the air before my young body hit the pavement, knocking me unconscious upon impact. My chin broke open and my leg bone was exposed where the car's right bumper had nicked it. My liver was lacerated as well. I was bleeding profusely in my stomach as I lay on the street in a pool of blood. My brother's arm was broken in 4 places, but when he saw me down and out, he ran to nearby homes trying to find help for me. I will eternally be grateful to him for that.

My dad was working outside in front of our house when the accident happened, and he heard the commotion in the distance. When he found out it was his boys who were hurt he rushed to the scene and found me still on the street. He told me later that God gave him the strength to pick me up. He cried for help, and some kind soul (maybe an angel in disguise) gave us a ride to the hospital. My brother was also en route to the hospital in another car.

I was rushed into emergency surgery, and doctors worked furiously trying to save my life. My aunt, Titi Violeta, was a doctor at the hospital that day, and she assisted in the surgery. After a little while she walked out of the surgical room for a few moments and told my dad, "Tony, they're losing Jorgito on the surgical table. If you know how to pray, ask God for a miracle." My dad was not a believer at the time and very far from the Lord, but in that moment he knelt in the hallway of that hospital and prayed, "God, if you're up there, if you can hear me, please save the life of my son. I promise to dedicate my life and my son's life to you if you bring him back to me." God heard his prayer and within seconds Titi Violeta came back out with incredible news, "Tony, the doctors were able to stabilize his condition."

Ninety-nine stitches later I was in one piece once again. God gave the surgeons wisdom and talent to not only put me together but to keep me functioning physically all these years as well. God is good and He is always near!

But the Lord of Heaven can go beyond the physical. God also provides emotional and psychological healing to those of us who need it. Nothing is too difficult for Him! His spiritual surgery mends the brokenhearted and pieces together and restores dreams, even after someone or something has shattered them.

Psalm 147 continues, "He counts the stars and calls them all by name. How great is our Lord! His power is absolute! His understanding is beyond comprehension!" (Psalm 147:4–5) This verse may seem out of order since the author first writes about God healing and bandaging the brokenhearted. What does a spiritually wounded person have to do with stars?

Well, consider that there are one hundred billion stars in our Milky Way galaxy and an estimated ten billion galaxies like ours in the universe. The thought that God knows the names of all those billions of stars is beyond comprehension. Now, consider that a large drop of water has as many molecules inside it as there are stars in the universe. God is mind-blowing in both the big and small things in life.

God's creation and His inexhaustible understanding chicken fries my cerebellum and scramble my medulla oblongata.

So then, since God's knowledge of the created universe is so amazing, how much more will He know about you and me and our circumstances and be able to heal those of us who are spiritually wounded?

God Knows...

You may feel like a speck of dust in a vast universe, yet God knows your name and everything about you. He says, "I knew you before I formed you in your mother's womb" (Jeremiah 1:5a).

God even knows how many hairs are on your head (Luke 12:7a). Even though the number of hairs on a person's head ranges anywhere from ninety thousand to one hundred fifty thousand, God knows the exact count for each person.[12]

God knows the secret dreams you keep under lock and key in your heart: "Take delight in the Lord, and he will give you the desires of your heart" (Psalm 37:4 NIV).

God knows those things that make you unique; "There was a huge man with six fingers on each hand and six toes on each foot—twenty-four in all. He also was descended from Rapha" (1Chronicles 20:6b NIV). Details!

The idea of God being able to take care of you begin to make sense when you consider how much He knows about you.

In the New Testament, the early Christians were afraid of a man with anger issues known as Saul of Tarsus. Saul was out to punish, incarcerate, and execute Christians. As he was on his way to Damascus to arrest some of Jesus's followers, the Bible says that Jesus Himself appeared to Saul in a bright, blinding light. The horse must have reared back; Saul fell to the ground. Then he heard Jesus's voice, "'Saul! Saul!

Why are you persecuting me?' 'Who are you, lord?' Saul asked. And the voice replied, 'I am Jesus, the one you are persecuting!'" (Acts 9:4b–5)

Saul was blinded on the spot! His companions had to lead him by the hand to Damascus. Saul was shocked, weakened, and helpless. He was in such a state of mind that he didn't eat or drink anything for three days; Saul was experiencing the darkness of his own soul. But God remained near.

Across town there was a believer by the name of Ananias who had no idea what had happened to Saul. God spoke to him too. "The Lord said, 'Go over to Straight Street, to the house of Judas. When you get there, ask for a man from Tarsus named Saul. He is praying to me right now. I have shown him a vision of a man named Ananias coming in and laying hands on him so he can see again'" (Acts 9:11–12).

God's knowledge is so specific. The Lord knew the street name and the owner of the house where Saul was staying. God was even aware of the thoughts and words Saul was directing to Him in his blindness.

God knows your country of residence, the city and state you live in, and the street and number of your house. He is keenly aware of your every thought and word. He knows the days you work and when you are off, what's on your agenda for the week, your hourly wage or salary, when you take your breaks, what you are going to do on vacation, and everything else in between. God's awareness of everything going on in our lives is both fascinating and comforting.

God was very aware of Saul's whereabouts. He called on Ananias to go pray for Saul, but Ananias did not think that was a logical idea. "Ananias protested, 'Master, you can't be serious. Everybody's talking about this man and the terrible things he's been doing, his reign of terror against your people in Jerusalem!'" (Acts 9:13a MSG)

In today's English, Ananias was asking, "Really, God? Really?" But God understood Ananias's fears and concerns, so He reassured this man, "But the Lord said, 'Go, for Saul is my chosen instrument to take my message to the Gentiles and to kings, as well as to the people of Israel. And I will show him how much he must suffer for my name's sake'" (Acts 9:15-16).

So Ananias obeyed! What happened next was nothing short of miraculous: "So Ananias went and found Saul. He laid his hands on him and said, 'Brother Saul, the Lord Jesus, who appeared to you on the road, has sent me so that you might regain your sight and be filled with the Holy Spirit.' Instantly something like scales fell from Saul's eyes, and he regained his sight. Then he got up and was baptized. Afterward he ate some food and regained his strength" (Acts 9:17–19).

And the rest is history! Saul, known to us as the apostle Paul, regained his sight and became the first and greatest missionary for the gospel of Jesus Christ the world has ever known. He also authored most of our New Testament Bible. Much of the depth of our Christian theology comes from his pen and ink.

The point I am trying to make is that the Lord knew everything there was to know about Saul and everything there was to know about Ananias, and He paired them together to bring His plan to life.

The BIG DEAL is that this wise, knowledgeable Lord and God we worship is the same God we read about in the Bible. He is mindful of your situation and is there to help you. Call on Him!

Sara had been attending our church for a while. Then she had a freak accident that left her with one of her legs broken in two places, her ankle shattered, and a couple of cracks in another bone. Doctors at the hospital had her immobilized with a wicked-looking contraption that had rods going all the way through her leg. They were waiting for the swelling to go down before they could surgically implant a metal plate and screws that would hold Sara's leg together again.

Sara is a massage therapist, and the day before the accident she had started a new job. When I went to her hospital bedside she was very discouraged. Her voice of reason, the heckler in her crowd at that moment, was filling her mind with negative thoughts: *You'll probably lose your job now; you won't have money to pay your rent and you'll lose your apartment. How are you going to go up the stairs of your third floor apartment; even if someone helps you by offering you a place to live, what are you going to do with Lily, your dog?*

When life takes a tumble, doesn't everything seem worse to you than it really is? Guard your mind! Most battles are won or lost up there.

Sara's mind was stripping her of whatever shred of hope she had left. She was devastated and growing increasingly desperate. I encouraged her to start listening to the voice of the Holy Spirit of God in her. Then we prayed together and I left, heavy-hearted. I went back to see her a few days later. Sara looked like a completely new woman.

She was still lying in the same bed awaiting surgery, but she now had a radiant disposition about her. What happened? She told me, "I didn't know what to do about my living arrangements and after we prayed I decided to look at my phone contact list. I came across the name of a person I have not seen or heard from for a couple of years. It's like God stopped me from pushing the scroll down button. He didn't want me to keep looking; He wanted me to call that one particular person."

The lady on the other end of the phone not only remembered Sara but also asked her and her dog to temporarily move in with her until she recovered from surgery. Hope was restored! Today Sara's life has turned around for the better. Her faith is stronger than ever. God knew her situation and was there to help her.

The wise man wrote, "For whoever finds me finds life and receives favor from the Lord" (Proverbs 8:35).

We all look for favor. We want God to give us the thumbs up. We seek His kindness and ask for Him to act in special ways toward us. The good news is that He loves you and me. The Lord wants to be like a loving father to every one of us who yield to Him.

Let's go back to the two things you listed earlier—those things you love and are passionate about. Mention both of them in prayer before the Lord. Remind the Lord about them often. Also imagine leaving those two passions, those motivations, in His able hands. Finally, wait and watch to see what God does. David wrote, "In the morning, LORD, you hear my voice; in the morning I lay my requests before you and wait expectantly" (Psalm 5:3 NIV).

A friend of mine, Linda, is madly in love with her husband, Doug. She's not quiet about it, either—Linda tells anyone who wants to know how great she thinks Doug is (he is a great guy, by the way). Linda has a passion for God as well.

Linda shared with our congregation how, before she met Doug, she had made a list of ten qualities she was looking for in a man. Her future husband was to be at least six feet tall with dark hair. She even confessed she wanted a man with thighs bigger than hers. Then she met Doug at an officers' club, and her first thought was, *this guy is old* (Doug is fourteen years older than she is). Doug did not meet even one of the qualities in Linda's top ten. But being a smooth operator, Doug invited her to slow dance. Linda told us that when she put her arms around him, she knew; God told her that this was His man for her. It didn't make any sense to her but it was, for all practical purposes, God's way to their happiness!

God knew her heart and paired her up with the man who would make her life incredibly satisfying and happy. So she swayed to the beat of her Heavenly Drummer. Doug and Linda have now been happily married for many years.

When I started my college career, I wanted to be a veterinarian. I love animals, and vets seem to make good money. I always wanted to help my folks financially so they could live well in the late stages of their lives. My parents didn't have much, so veterinary medicine became my target. Then I failed my first college science class, biology.

My heart was broken as I realized that a career in veterinary medicine was not for me. I then decided to pursue a degree in business administration, but could not pass accounting. I left college and enrolled in a school to learn auto mechanics, but failed miserably when I had to take an engine apart and put it back together again. I had so many nuts and bolts left after the thing was together that I unscrewed the oil pan and hid them all there. I once again enrolled in the University of Central Florida (Go Knights!) and began to sense the Lord calling me into a full time Christian vocation. I was able to earn a college degree in foreign language education (Spanish) and went on to pursue a career in ministry.

Trust me, the last thing in my mind when I was growing up was to be involved in anything religious. My parents were not church-going people when I was a child. Knowledge of God and religion had not flowed through my veins until I gave my heart to Jesus Christ as my Savior when I was an older teenager. So the thought of getting a master's degree in theology and becoming a preacher was the farthest thing from my mind. But God had a plan!

So I made my decision to follow the Heavenly Drummer's beat. My bride, the love of my life, felt the same way, and twenty days after getting married we packed everything we owned into our Pontiac Sunbird and moved to New Orleans. That was over thirty years ago.

Looking back through the mountaintops and valleys of ministry, my bride and I agree that we would do it all over again!

Follow your passion! Live at the beat of His drum. And always remember that He is near!

What's Your Take?

1. Near the beginning of this chapter Pastor Jorge challenged us to write down two things we are passionate about. Would you mind sharing what you wrote?

2. How do you spot a genuinely excited Christian? Name a trait or something you would see in someone (other than a T-shirt that reads, "I love Jesus!") that would make you wonder if that person is a born-again believer.

3. When you read that God bandages the brokenhearted and heals their wounds, what comes to mind? Would you be willing to share an experience when you felt the Lord pick you up and put you back together?

4. Pastor Jorge described God's grand universe above us and the vastness of a microscopic world that's invisible to the eye. What blows your mind most about God's creation?

5. When you read that the Lord carefully put you together in your mother's womb and that He knows everything about you, how does that make you feel?

6. How certain are you that God knows everything about you: your work schedule, your favorite TV shows, where you go on vacation, your dreams and hopes, etc.? Are you sure you believe God knows?

7. What is the best way to guard our minds?

PART 4

Still to Come...

8

When Age Becomes a Heckler

Never stop laughing. People who
stop laughing grow old fast!

ONE NIGHT AFTER I turned forty, my youngest daughter and I were in the hotel pool while on vacation on the west side of Florida. I looked up and was amazed by four moving objects in the dark sky above. I looked at Sara, concerned, and said, "You're not going to believe this, but I think there are four UFOs way up over our heads!" She immediately looked up, excited. "Where, where?" I pointed directly over us. "Right there. Right above us." Again she asked, "Where, Dad?" I pointed again. "Right there above our heads." Puzzled, she asked, "Are you ok, Dad? There's nothing up there but one lonely star." I squinted. "Right over us, you don't see those four little moving dots?" "No... there's one star. Dad, you need glasses." Then for the first time it hit me: *My eyes are going bad. I'm getting old.* I was deflated. Saddened.

Some time back I was sitting at lunch with Sara and a couple of her friends. One of them was about to have her twenty-third birthday. I offered my congratulations, but with a genuine frown on her face she groaned, "I don't want to get old!" Really? At twenty-three? I guess we have this negative perspective that growing old is a bad thing.

Ok, so physically speaking our bodies do begin to break down with age. At forty you need glasses. Ten years later you need the dreaded colonoscopy. YIKES!

Minutes before I had mine done, the anesthesiologist came by my bedside and asked, "Mr. Acevedo, why are you doing this procedure?" I answered, "I don't know man. Get me out of here!" But there was nothing he could do. Around noontime they rolled me into the surgical room and a nurse said, "I'll bet you're hungry." I said, "All I can think about is going to Don's Famous Hoagies after this." Then a mean sounding nurse uttered the six words no man ever wants to hear, "Please turn on your side, sir." I shielded my posterior with my hand. "Wait a minute, let's talk about it, we don't really have to do this!" But by that time I was defenseless. My right finger was clipped to something that lit it up like *ET*. One arm had an IV, my other arm was attached to the blood pressure machine and my chest had little round things glued to it with wires attached. The anesthesiologist then injected something wonderful into my IV. The last thing I remember saying was, "Dude this is powerful stuff…" The next moment I was out for one of the best sleeps I have ever had.

By the way, there are two reasons why I had a colonoscopy done: First, my wife inspired me. She was fearless when she had to do hers. Second, when we initially went to see her doctor about it she told us that since they have been doing colonoscopies, colon cancer deaths have been reduced by 70 percent! When I heard those figures, I said, "Sign me up, Doc!"

The Gloom of Doom

Other than physical problems, though, who says that getting old is a bad thing? The heckler in your crowd does, that's who, and so does almost everyone else! Society tells us to slow down before we break down. But how did we come to dread getting old? The media has a lot to do with it.

We have been trained to think that beauty is indeed only skin deep and that it has to do with fewer wrinkles, less fat, and less sagging. So we use anti-aging creams, hair coloring, cosmetic surgery… there's nothing wrong with any of those, of course, if they make you feel better about yourself. I'm just stating the fact that in the twenty-first century, the constant message we receive is that we must do whatever we can to stay forever young.

Some will do anything to stay young looking including Botox injections and face and neck lifts. Other extreme treatments sound absolutely ridiculous. People apply blood-sucking leeches to certain parts of their bodies, rub kitty litter all over their bodies, and spread hemorrhoid cream under their eyes to minimize the bags. But the most disgusting treatment I've heard of is rubbing bird droppings all over the face to cleanse, smooth, and brighten the skin pores (a well-known Japanese spa treatment).

We have bought into the thinking that beauty is strictly external and that getting old is unacceptable.

We do not like the idea of getting old because we have also seen our older loved ones battle dreaded diseases. I typed the word 'aging' into my browser to see where the Internet would take me, and it showed me a list of related topics: Alzheimer's, dementia, obesity, skin problems—how depressing! No wonder we don't want to go there.

Recently during a Sunday sermon I mentioned that growing old is really not that bad. I reminded the congregation that the fifties are the new thirties, the sixties the new forties, and that the seventies are the new fifties. A well-advanced in age senior worshipping with us that morning blurted out—purposely or not—"Who are you kidding, Pastor?" To her, aging is not fun and games.

One word describes the idea of getting older: DOOMSDAY! We fear that Social Security and pensions may go dry. We are told to hoard non-perishables because of a coming economic collapse and to beware of global warming. We are made aware of enemy threats and the menace of new diseases, and the prospect of the future becomes demoralizing.

"What if", we ask ourselves, "when I get old I am pushed aside into a corner and left there?" Scary thought! A senior told me recently, "Pastor, the golden years are really not that golden. They look more like the color of rust!"

Old age is still to come for many of us, but as I get older I refuse to believe that the good old days are behind me. These are the most exciting days to be alive! The past is not where the best of times are buried; the present and future are where the thrills are found. If you like to create, your best idea is yet to be born. If you're an author, your best story is yet to be written. If you're a preacher, like me, your best sermon is yet to be preached. If you're an athlete, your best game is yet to be played! You've got to believe that!

In his book, *Been There. Done That. Now What?* Dr. Ed Young tells the story of S. L. Potter. Mr. Potter bungee-jumped for the first time at age one hundred. His kids were opposed to it but disregarding their concerns Mr. Potter climbed up a very high tower and jumped. His first words when he was off the cord? "Give me back my teeth!"[13]

Make sure you live each day as if it was your last!

Don't listen to your heckler within telling you that you're through because of age.

The Beauty of Becoming

In 2002, a horse named War Emblem was running in the Belmont Stakes in hopes of being the twelfth horse in the history of horse racing to win the coveted Triple Crown. But War Emblem stumbled at the gate. As the race came to a close, the horse faded into the rest of the field to finish in eighth place.

As you read this you may be stumbling at the gate of your twilight years. You feel like you are fading as old age creeps in. To silence your heckler, let God renew your mind. Let Him transform the way you think. The apostle Paul wrote, "Don't be like the people of this world, but let God change the way you think. Then you will know how to do everything that is good and pleasing to him" (Romans 12:2 CEV).

The Greek word *metamorphosis* translates into English word *change*—a transforming physiological change. It's what happens when a tadpole becomes a frog or when a rough-looking, slow-moving caterpillar turns into a colorful and beautiful flying butterfly.

The Lord wants to transform the way you think, filter whatever depressing ideas you have about your present or future, and replace those ideas with His Word so you can enjoy life to the full. His Holy Spirit wants to help you see from His point of view that God is not through with you yet. Trust me, when God is through with you He will call you home to Heaven. Until then He wants to use you regardless of your life stage.

Stop listening to the heckler of age. Finish strong! Believe that your best is yet to come. I was inspired by something Dave Ramsey wrote in his book *Entreleadership*. He has observed that people who continue working hard and pursuing their dreams during their fifties become more productive and financially stronger than at any other time in their lives.[14]

Age should never be the fading factor of your life. Leo Goodwin founded GEICO at the age of 50.[15] While facing a divorce at 52 Carol Gardner decided to get a British bulldog as a pet. At Christmas time she immersed her dog Zelda in a bubble bath, put a Santa hat and a fake bubble beard on her and took a picture. Carol mailed it to her friends as a Christmas card and they all fell in love with it. That was the beginning of what is known today as Zelda Wisdom, a multimillion-dollar greeting card industry.[16]

Resist the temptation of being pessimistic about your future. Silence that heckler! Moses gives us this perspective, "Teach us to number our days, that we may gain a heart of wisdom" (Psalm 90:12 NIV).

In other words, count them—and make them count. Your tombstone is going to have the day, month, and year you were born and a little dash, followed by the day, month, and year you died. What happens during that dash is your concern.

Life is short. Enjoy it! Be wise and live out loud for God.

The author did not say, "Teach us to number our years," which is how we usually measure our lives and times. He breaks it down to days, because every day you and I have twenty-four hours to live life to the fullest, to take a step forward, to better ourselves, to do something of value for someone else (which always makes us feel good about ourselves). Every day we have a chance to make a memory, to squeeze the juice out of moments with our loved ones. Every day we also have an opportunity to make a difference for God's kingdom.

As You Get Older

Rethink getting old! As you age, don't worry about the uncertainties and insecurities you may have.

Jesus said, "You cannot add any time to your life by worrying about it…So don't worry about tomorrow, because tomorrow will have its own worries. Each day has enough trouble of its own" (Matthew 6:27, 34 NCV).

In other words, it will do you no good to pace back and forth agonizing over something you fear. You can develop ulcers that way.

Is it not true that most things we worry about seldom come to pass?

For example, I live by the Atlantic coast. The number one thing most people worry about when going to the beach is being eaten by a shark. But that rarely happens. Actually, according to Jeff Corwin, anytime you're in the water at a beach in Florida there's probably a shark nearby. However, the chance of being killed by a shark is one in 264 million.[17]

In the book *Strengthening Your Grip* Pastor and author Charles Swindoll writes, "View life as a challenge, not as a threat."[18]

Do not waste time worrying about those things out of your control; instead, pray over them. Give them to the Lord and let Him deal with all of it. Trust that the Lord is able to do what seems impossible!

The seniors I know who remain excited about life are the ones staying active and doing the things they know they can do. Many of the beloved Bible passages you know involve folks who were aging. Four of them come to mind right away.

Consider the great story of Ruth. Through an amazing series of circumstances, the struggling young widow met and married the wealthy man by the name of Boaz and their first child became an ancestor of the Savior, Jesus Christ. It's a great romance story. You can read that whole Bible book in less than an hour.

You may ask, "Where is there an aging person in that story?" Naomi, Ruth's mother-in-law, was an aging widow. She encouraged Ruth to work in a field. She instructed her to stay around Boaz. Then one evening Naomi coached Ruth to bathe, smell good, and look sharp when she met Boaz. The man melted like butter in her presence and their lives changed forever.

Naomi had been a bitter woman because her husband and sons had died young, but God orchestrated events in her life to once again make her feel happy and blessed.

Next, think about the directions Paul wrote to Titus concerning the aged in his congregation, "Similarly, teach the older women to live in a way that honors God…they should teach others what is good. These older women must train the younger women to love their husbands and their children, to live wisely and be pure, to work in their homes, to do good, and to be submissive to their husbands. Then they will not bring shame on the word of God" (Titus 2:3–5).

Paul is saying that even when you're older there's work to be done. Your influence doesn't stop with age; it gets stronger because of the wisdom and experience you've gained through the years.

A third example is that of the apostle John. He was probably in his late eighties or early nineties when he was exiled to a rugged, bare island called Patmos. From there John wrote letters to churches encouraging them and telling them about the end times. Those letters are included in the Book of Revelation.

In those days, before the invention of computers and the Internet (yes, there were days like that), while facing difficult conditions, John did more than pray for the Church. He was actively writing about God's plans to seven churches near the island he was confined to.

Once done with the writing, John had to rely on someone to get the letters and transport them via boat, then by horseback or on foot to each of their destinations. Despite all those difficulties, the Holy Spirit used John to teach us amazing things. We are seeing many of these prophecies come to pass before our very eyes. We all are so glad that John didn't hold back from writing just because he was old. He challenged himself.

As you get older, challenge yourself! Silence your heckler by continuing to dream big about what God may do with your life. Stay passionate. Do those things you are able to do, and refuse to dwell on those things you can't do anymore. Zechariah is a prime example of this.

Zechariah was an older priest of God's temple in Israel some two thousand years ago. The Bible describes him as one who was well along in years. One day while he was doing his priestly duties, the angel Gabriel appeared to him with a message from above. God wanted Zechariah to do a new work, to father a son who would later become the Savior's frontrunner. You and I know his son as John the Baptist.

This was going to be a challenge for Zechariah and his wife Elizabeth. Not only were they full-blown seniors, they had not been able to have children. She was barren. Zechariah had prayed for the Lord to open her womb and let her have children, but the answer had not yet come. Regardless and however, God had an amazing job for Zechariah late in life.

You would have thought that Zechariah was jumping for joy over answered prayers, but that is not the way it happened. Rather than believing God and listening to the sweet words of the angel, Zechariah chose to listen to the bitter words of his age heckler. "Zechariah said to the angel, 'How can I know that what you say is true? I am an old man, and my wife is old, too'" (Luke 1:18 NCV).

What a waste of a great time to celebrate! Because of Zechariah's unbelief, the angel muted the man for the nine months of Elizabeth's pregnancy. That could have been avoided had he just said, "I believe!"

Why do we think of old age as synonymous with inactivity? God is through with us only when we breathe our last. There is still work to be done for His kingdom and for your enjoyment.

The heckler of age will tell you that you are through. Garbage! Challenge yourself anyway. You don't have to bungee jump. Just follow the creative ideas your brain is churning up. There is plenty more for you to do. Silence your heckler. Move forward, and have a blast while great things happen!

What's Your Take?

1. How would you define "old?"
2. What do you fear most about getting old? When you think about dreaded diseases, which one concerns you most?
3. The author mentioned a man who bungee jumped at the age of one hundred. Money not being a hindrance, what crazy, wild thing would you do if you had the courage for it?
4. Read Genesis 25:7–8. How does your Bible translation describe the sum of Abraham's life, and how would you translate that into twenty-first century lingo?
5. Sometimes people well advanced in years begin to express regrets about events in their lives. What do you think are the most common regrets people have at death? What is the best way to deal with regrets?
6. How do you think God could transform your thinking about growing old?
7. What can you do to prepare for growing old?

9

The Heckler from the Great Beyond

For to me, to live is Christ and to die is gain!

THE APOSTLE PAUL[19]

Death is not the end of your story but the
beginning of a chapter that is yet to be written.

YEARS AGO I was asked to perform a funeral for a small child who had
died of Sudden Infant Death Syndrome (SIDS). I did not know the
couple prior to this. The young parents didn't speak any English, so
the funeral home director called me to see if I could help. I was more
than willing. It was a very sad time, as children's funerals always are.
The couple was devastated.

They requested we have a short graveside service after the funeral.
When it was over I told the couple that it was best for them not to stay
around for the lowering of the casket and burial, but they refused.
The sound of dirt hitting the tiny casket several feet beneath us in
that freshly dug hole is forever in my mind. After a while I once again
gave the couple my condolences and went my way.

A few weeks later I received a phone call from the young mother. Her husband had been arrested. She told me that he had not been able to deal with losing his child and had blamed her for the tragedy. She recounted that every day the man would go and sit by his son's graveside to burn a candle. He would sit there alone for hours. Then one day he lost his mind.

He went home and became violent with his wife, and the police were called to the domestic disturbance. Still in a rage, he fought the officers. He even bit off one of the officers' fingers. The man was apprehended and later deported back to his home country. Death had become a heckler in his crowd.

Death has been called all kinds of names: the grave, the great beyond, the underworld, the grim reaper, the final frontier, and others. Regardless of what you call it, death has a way of messing with our minds and emotions like nothing else can. And because of the seeming finality of it, the death of a loved one threatens to slow us down and hold us back.

After thirty-plus years of ministry and dealing with people, it has been my experience that death has the potential to ruin the lives of those left behind. Thoughts like, *Why did this happen?* or *I can't go on without him or her* or *I have nothing to live for now* can have devastating, long-term effects if not dealt with correctly.

The Promises

Death is a heckler that must be silenced, but how? The answer is Jesus Christ! He overcame death with His resurrection. Just like He came back to life, so shall all who call on His name. When our ultimate opponent takes the life of someone we love, the only hope we have to hold on to, our only certainty, is that all who believe in Christ will literally continue to live up in heaven. Jesus made a promise to His followers, "I am the resurrection and the life; he who believes in Me will live even if he dies" (John 11:25 NASB).

You must believe with all of your heart that heaven is not some fantasyland in a children's story that someone dreamed up. Heaven, according to the One who created all things, is a tangible place with people and buildings and landscape and scenery and activity and music and worship.

Jesus's disciples were saddened over the idea of the Master dying. But the Lord encouraged them by saying, "Let not your heart be troubled; you believe in God, believe also in Me. In My Father's house are many mansions; if it were not so, I would have told you. I go to prepare a place for you. And if I go and prepare a place for you, I will come again and receive you to Myself; that where I am, there you may be also" (John 14:1–3 NKJV).

In other words, Jesus was saying something like, "I'm not lying to you. There is an actual place still to come, My Dad's heavenly house. I'm going there to build you a place you can call your own so we can be together forever."

Keep in mind that Jesus was not into telling tall tales. He was Truth incarnate! What He said either happened in the past, is happening today, or will happen in the future.

You may say, "I'm not sure how much I believe there is a place called heaven after death." Of course you are entitled to your own opinion. However, Truth is not dependent on whether you believe it or not. Truth stands on its own merit.

One of Jesus's disciples, Thomas, was not present when Jesus first appeared to the others after His glorious resurrection. When Peter and the rest of them told Thomas about it he thought they were full of bologna. And he was emphatic about it, "I won't believe it unless I see the nail wounds in his hands, put my fingers into them, and place my hand into the wounds of his side" (John 20:25b).

But Jesus had indeed come back from the grave. The next time He appeared before His disciples, He went straight to Thomas and offered the holes in His hands and side for Thomas to do what he said he would…of course Thomas didn't.

That same Jesus who defeated death said that there is a heaven and that it is ours for the taking. When your believing husband, wife, or loved one dies, you can be certain that person will come to life again, as Jesus did, and that you will be with him or her again in that perfect place. That kind of faith silences your heckler from the great beyond and helps you survive the tough times.

Consider a verse in the most beloved of all psalms, "Even though I walk through the valley of the shadow of death, I fear no evil, for You are with me; Your rod and Your staff, they comfort me" (Psalm 23:4 NASB).

David is telling us that death is a passing stage in life, something we all have to walk through one day (unless Jesus returns first). A key to silencing the heckler of death is to remember that death is a walk-through and not a place for loved ones to stop and grieve for too long. Your hope and mine, your certainty (my certainty) is Jesus and heaven!

We also learn from that one verse that God is near the grief-stricken. He is there when we need Him most, by our side; so close that if we could see it His shadow would be covering us.

A long time ago I heard someone say that God may whisper in our triumphs but uses a megaphone during our tragedies. Reach out to Him! With His help, you will slowly but surely begin to move forward again.

I have known people who went through a tough loss and yet were able to rise in victory over their difficult circumstances. I have Christian friends who were devastated by the tragic death of a child or by the loss of a spouse of many years. The tears were real. The nights agonizing. The pain almost unbearable. We all have gone through various degrees of grief because of loved ones gone. But God stands Tall in the middle of our hurt and gives peace and hope.

Believers know, without a shadow of doubt, that just as Jesus resurrected, so shall we! Death cannot stop this life the Lord has given us. It is an open doorway to a beginning of something new and better waiting for us on the other side.

David was known as a man after God's own heart (Acts 13:22). One of his valleys of the shadow of death involved his young son dying. It was an agonizing time for David. He prayed and fasted and begged God to heal the child, but nothing worked. After the child's death David got up, washed up, and went on with life. He was asked about it and, "David replied, "I fasted and wept while the child was alive, for I said, 'Perhaps the LORD will be gracious to me and let the child live.' But why should I fast when he is dead? Can I bring him back again? I will go to him one day, but he cannot return to me" (2Samuel 12:22–23).

David believed his child was safe in heaven and that he would see him again. O what a happy reunion it will be when we get to see our loved ones again!

The Zoo of God

The place the Lord has created for those who love Him, our future home, must be an amazing kind of place! It made the apostle Paul write, "For to me, to live is Christ and to die is gain" (Philippians 1:21 NIV).

Our humanness argues, "But how can dying be a gain and not a loss?" The answer is that heaven is an absolutely incredible place beyond our finite human understanding.

My first time snorkeling was in Honduras. I couldn't believe all the bright neon colors of fish and coral. Everywhere I looked there was something new and inspiring. Then, after swimming in the shallows for a while, I found myself in deeper waters. I almost gasped as the underwater world opened up. I can only describe it as an underwater canyon with big fish on the very bottom. My breathing and heartbeat became faster and my eyes opened wide because of the excitement of the moment. I believe that is how we will feel when we get to heaven.

When our eyes finally close for the last time down here they will open wide up there. Our mouths will also open and remain that way as we take in the impressive colors and shocking beauty of Jesus' creation up in heaven. We may say, "This can't be. Am I dreaming?" But our new home will be better than a dream. We will be in awe of the landscape and high mountains of heaven (Revelation 21:10). There are fruit trees there (Revelation 22:1), and a river (Revelation 22:2), and places to live that make the most amazing homes on earth seem like little shacks (John 14:1-3).

Imagine the best, most amazing, and most fun and you're beginning to get it. All things are possible with God! (Mark 10: 27). Heaven has no limits.

How do you imagine heaven will be? STOP READING for a few moments and get into a dreaming session about heaven. What do you see with the eyes of your mind?

One night I asked my Wednesday night small group, "What do you wish you will be able to do in heaven?" There were no limits to their answers. My dear friend Naderah said, "I want to be able to sing like Barbara Streisand and play the piano like Liberace." My buddy Jim answered, "I want to be able to go explore Alpha Centauri and around the whole universe." Then my pal Graydon said, "I want to have cows in heaven and take care of them." I do not see why any of those things would not happen.

I remember Billy Graham saying one time that God knows what heaven is going to be for you and that He is going to make it all happen.

Some people (my family included) believe that part of heaven will be seeing their pets again. Pet lovers consider their animals as part of the family. God totally understands that! In fact, God inspired the prophet Nathan to portray to King David the love relationship that can exist between a man and a pet. In this particular case, the man had a little lamb, "He raised it, and it grew up with him and his children. It shared his food, drank from his cup and even slept in his arms. It was like a daughter to him" (2Samuel 12:3b NIV).

That tells me that God understands what pets mean to us. Through the years I have been asked many times by pet owners if I think they will see their beloved animals again. My answer is always and without hesitation, "YES!" Not only because of that Bible verse, but also because when the beloved disciple John referred to the living creatures he saw before the throne of God in heaven, he used a Greek word that translates into our English word *zoo*. The zoo of God, the whole creation of God, is up there! John wrote, "The first of these living beings was like a lion; the second was like an ox; the third had a human face; and the fourth was like an eagle in flight" (Revelation 4:7).

The lion represents wild animals, the ox domesticated animals (pets included), the eagle winged animals, and the human face, us, Homo sapiens. All of God's creation will be there.

The prophet Isaiah described part of heaven as having animals. "The wolf will live with the lamb, the leopard will lie down with the goat, the calf and the lion and the yearling together; and a little child will lead them. The cow will feed with the bear, their young will lie down together, and the lion will eat straw like the ox. The infant will play near the cobra's den, and the young child will put its hand into the viper's nest. They will neither harm nor destroy on all my holy mountain, for the earth will be filled with the knowledge of the LORD as the waters cover the sea" (Isaiah 11:6–9 NIV).

Isaiah repeats this later: "The wolf and the lamb will feed together, and the lion will eat straw like the ox, and dust will be the serpent's food. They will neither harm nor destroy on all my holy mountain,' says the LORD" (Isaiah 65:25 NIV).

I realize those references have to do with Jesus's one-thousand-year reign of peace on earth. But the millennial kingdom of Christ will be part of the heavenly experience!

Some may have issues with my ideas of animals in heaven, but the bottom line is that no one has already been to heaven and experienced all there is to enjoy there except for the Lord Jesus. All ideas can be subject to discussion. I am just saying that Scripture tells us there will be animals in heaven and I prefer to have the hope that I am going to see my beloved pets again.

In his amazing book called *Heaven,* Randy Alcorn quotes a poem by theologian John Piper. In it Pastor Piper describes the incredibly joyous moment of seeing his beloved pet *Blackie* in heaven for the first time. She is galloping through the beautiful landscape until she leaps to the place where he is.[20]

Oh, the bliss, the blessedness of being in heaven one day! The Lord Jesus described heaven as a place of laughter (Luke 6:21 NIV) and I can see myself in a mix of total relaxation and euphoria as I am attacked and licked by my tail-wagging dogs. What a great day that will be.

Your Kind of Place

My dad had been married to Mom for nearly forty years. He had been a great husband to his wife and father to my brother and me. My dad loved Jesus and studying the Bible with all his heart. He read incessantly and was very educated in Bible history and doctrine. I considered him my resident theologian. Dad had earned an Associate of Ministry degree through the mail from the New Orleans Baptist Theological Seminary and become the pastor of a Spanish mission church in Orlando, Florida.

Just before turning sixty-two, he started doing weird things. He would sing an old hymn at church alongside everyone else but he would use a different tune from the one being played by the musicians. But because Dad had a great sense of humor, Mom did not think much of it.

Then one day Dad was sweeping the floor at home by tucking the broom under one arm because the other side of his body seemed to be temporarily paralyzed. Mom took him to the hospital. Tests revealed that he had a malignant, inoperable tumor in his brain. After the biopsy, the doctor told Mom that her beloved husband only had three months to live at most. We were all devastated.

While Dad rested in the surgical recovery room after the biopsy, Mom came to me and said, "Son, you have to tell your dad that he is dying." I obviously bucked at the idea. "Why me?" "Because you're the minister in the family." I was not willing to play that card and told her that I would decide when we went to see him a few minutes later.

When Mom and I got to Dad's room she stood on one side of the bed while I stood on the other and I asked him how he was feeling. With a bright smile that is forever imprinted in my brain, he said, "I feel great, son! I don't think the doctor found anything wrong with me and that he is going to send me home. I'm pretty sure I'm alright." At that time I felt compelled to tell Dad the truth. With courage and strength that I can only attribute as God-given, I looked at him in the eyes and said, "Dad, we met with the doctor and he told us that he found a large, inoperable, malignant tumor in your brain. He told us that you only have three months to live."

For what seemed like an eternity, Dad stared at me silently as if he had not heard a single word. So I repeated myself. "Dad, did you not hear me? The doctor said there's nothing he can do for you and you only have three months to live." He once again briefly stared at me and in a calm voice he answered, "I heard you son." He paused for a moment and continued, "I have served the Lord faithfully for many years and I'm ready to go to heaven." He then turned his face toward Mom, stared at her for a moment, and started singing a church *corito* (a short Spanish gospel/Christian song) about the love of God and heaven. Mom immediately joined Dad and in that precious moment, while looking at each other, they encouraged each other and celebrated God with peaceful hearts.

Time stood still! Heaven had become so real for both of them. Dad wasn't trying to be a tough *macho-man* in the face of adversity. He was just acting on the hope that born-again believers have concerning the afterlife.

The next three months of Dad's life proved to be very difficult indeed, but in the end, when death—the heckler from the great beyond—made some noise, it was quickly quieted by the victory tune we all have in Christ.

For the people of God, death is not the end of the story but the beginning of a new chapter in their book yet to be written. The end of your earthly life begins a new heavenly life for you. It is the reason Paul wrote, "And now, dear brothers and sisters, we want you to know what will happen to the believers who have died so you will not grieve like people who have no hope." (1Thessalonians 4:13).

The born-again are not exempt from pain and hurt. Expressing grief is healthy and therapeutic. But unlike people without Jesus Christ in their hearts, people who are hopeless when a loved one dies, even in our tears there is this hope and certainty that just as Jesus lived after His death, so shall we who believe.

The Bible also shows us that we will know each other in the afterlife (Luke 16:19–31; Mark 9:2–6). I will see my dad again and my mom and my brother Hector and my sister-in-law Charmagne and my grandma *Abu* and my mother-in-law Donna and my brother-in-law David and my wife's brother-in-law George and all the other people I know who loved Jesus the way I do.

I once performed a funeral for a widow I did not know. She was Spanish and did not have a church home, so the funeral director called me and paired us up. I met her and shared Jesus with her at her home. I told her that He is the Way, the Truth, and the Life (John 14:6). But she remained lost in grief and hopeless. On the day of the funeral I saw her do something I had never seen anyone do before. She leaned over into the casket next to her deceased husband and had her picture taken with him. What gloomy misery!

It has been said that death is a necessary evil we all must go through to get to the other side. But we hold to the truth that when our spirit is away from this body, it is at home with the Lord (2Corinthians 5:8).

Our transition from earth to heaven is instant. After you take your last gulp of air on this planet, your very next breath will happen in paradise. Not a moment passes. The transition is smooth! Perfect! Glorious!

During Jesus's hours on the cross, one of the criminals crucified next to the Lord said, "Jesus, remember me when you come into your kingdom" (Luke 23:42).

Just before death, the man turned to the Lord for the salvation of his soul, and Jesus welcomed him. "And He said to him, 'Truly I say to you, today you shall be with Me in Paradise'" (Luke 23:43 NASB).

The term *paradise* that Jesus used referred to a pleasure-filled, walled-in garden or park.

Think of a place in nature you want to go to and relax. That is paradise. Think of a picnic under a tree by the river's edge with your sweetie; that's paradise. Think of taking your kids to a beautiful park where they can run and play; that's paradise.

The kid in me loves to imagine. I compare paradise to the place in the movie when Mary Poppins takes the kids and her pal Bert through a sidewalk picture at the park. All of a sudden they all find themselves in this amazing new world where they can ride merry-go-round horses through the countryside, a place where they can have tea and cakes served by singing penguins.

You may think I'm ridiculous, but you haven't been there to prove me wrong. I am just comparing the place Jesus made for His followers to a place of utmost fun and happiness.

What is heaven going to be like for you? What will you see? Whom will you meet?

Sailing Away

During funerals I like to illustrate the continuation of a Christian's life after death to a sailboat.

Imagine for a moment that you are by the shore of the Atlantic Ocean in Miami, Florida. You are just chilling on South Beach. Several yards away from you in the ocean there's a beautiful white sailboat at anchor. You're taking in some sunrays, thinking: *It would be nice to be in that boat right now.* Then, just as that thought passes through your mind, people from the cabin underneath emerge and start working on deck as if ready to set sail. Soon they lift anchor and start moving away from the shore. You're watching this action unfold and you wonder if they're heading to the Bahamas. You are wowed by it all and say to yourself, "Please take me with you. I don't want to go back to the office tomorrow."

In moments the wind fills the sail, making that boat start cutting swiftly through the waves. As minutes go by, the sailboat moves farther away from you, its silhouette becoming smaller and smaller to your sight until you're squinting to pick it up in the far horizon. Finally it disappears from sight. Has it vanished? Disappeared into oblivion? Absolutely not! It's still sailing even though you can't see it.

That's what happens to born-again believers at death. We move on to a better place. We hold on to that belief with every fiber of our being. Eternity with God and our loved ones is something we must eagerly anticipate. Looking forward to that great reunion helps silence the death-heckler.

Sometimes there is no answer for why death happens for people who are still full of life. The death heckler will use the seeming unfairness of someone dying early. It will throw that in your face and tell you that God doesn't care about you or your family and friends. If you choose to listen to that voice, it will draw you further and further away from the One who loves you more than words can describe. Silence that heckler by considering the goodness of God.

When my brother Hector went home to heaven he had just celebrated his fifty-seventh birthday. My brother was young and the kind of guy who loved life. He had a beautiful family and great friends. Hector was also enjoying the fruits of being a successful businessman. His employees loved him dearly. But cancer got ahold of him, and though he fought a good fight, it finally took his life. My brother went through many difficult times and some horrible days. But I am thankful that the instant Hector breathed his last on earth he was fully restored in heaven. Healed!

My family and I arrived at Houston, Texas, the very day Hector went to heaven. A few days later we were all getting ready for the memorial service. In the midst of all that turmoil, the ultimate heckler from the great beyond kept popping a question in my mind, *Why didn't God do something for your brother? If He is so powerful and good, how is it that He allowed this to happen?* Trust me; it's easy to give in to that kind of thinking. I certainly do not have the answers to those questions, but I want to share with you some thoughts I shared at my brother's funeral that I hope will be help you if you happen to be going through the difficulty of the death of a loved one at this time:

"I know the prevailing question in most people's minds who knew Hector is, *Why?* Why didn't God do something for my brother? Why didn't he heal him? Why didn't the Lord take the cancer away? I'm not sure of the answers to those questions, but I want to share with you that God did do something for Hector. He did something for Hector on a hill called Calvary two thousand years ago. That's the place Roman soldiers led Jesus to and nailed Him to the cross for our sins. The Bible says that God is love. He loves you and me and Hector so much that He was willing to send His Son Jesus Christ to pay the penalty of our sins. The Bible says that Jesus died there, but three days later He rose from the dead to give us life. Jesus said that anyone who believes in Him will live even though they die. Hector had given his heart to Jesus Christ; he was a follower, so the Lord has given him eternal life through the forgiveness of sins. God may not have healed my brother in a miraculous way on earth, but He did something for Hector on a hill called Calvary a long time ago.

Second, God did something for Hector in a place called heaven. Hector is in a better place today. And that is not just a phrase we Christians use when we have nothing else to say about someone who dies. Hector is fully alive in heaven today. Heaven is real. As real and solid as this church we are in and those pews you are sitting on.

The night Jesus was arrested, the disciples were saddened by His talk about betrayal and death. Then Jesus said to them something like, and I am paraphrasing, "Do not let your hearts be shaken over this. Trust Me. In my Father's house are many mansions; I'm not lying to you. I've been there and I'm going back to fix you a spot there so we can be together forever" (taken from John 14:1-3).

By now Hector has already been given a key to a brand new mansion. He has also received a new heavenly body, and a great big happy family reunion is already taking place. By this time Hector has already met Dad, Mom, and *Abu*. And listen, there are all kinds of things to do up there. If you thought we are all going to be sitting on clouds strumming a harp, you just don't understand the wonders of what the future holds in the afterlife. Hector is alright! Life in heaven is so good! And, I believe that even if he were given a chance to come back here, he wouldn't want to.

Hector may not be here in person, but he is fully alive right now. After my brother breathed his last here, the very next gulp of air he took was up there. By faith you've got to believe that!"

At that time I'm pretty sure I shared the sailboat illustration I described earlier in this chapter. After that I continued,

"Jesus did something for Hector on a hill called Calvary and the Lord already did something for Hector in a place called heaven, but I believe Jesus is doing something for you right now in a secret place called your heart. It is there that you long for seeing my brother again…and we will see Hector again. Jesus promised we would. If you've given your heart to Jesus as Hector did you will meet him again. The Bible tells us that we are going to know each other in heaven. For that reason, all of a sudden, heaven has a new ring to it. It's a sweeter place because he is there. We are going to see Hector again!"

I wanted everyone there to know the certainty I carry in my heart because the Bible tells me so. The heckler from the great beyond will make you question and doubt at times, but you will shut him up when, by faith, you believe God has acted through His Son, Jesus, on your behalf.

To overcome the heckler from the great beyond, you must believe the best is yet to come. If you and I could take a peek into a window that looks toward heaven, I believe we would see all kinds of wonderful activity happening. Death is not the end of the story; it is the beginning. You remind the heckler about that and you will overcome!

What's Your Take?

1. Put yourself in the sandals of all the friends of Jesus. Use one-word answers to describe how you felt on that weekend when Jesus died and came back to life.
2. Pastor Jorge shares what some of his friends said they would like to do when they get to heaven. How about you? Thinking of heaven as a place of unlimited possibilities, what would you like to do there?
3. Who do you look forward to seeing up in heaven?
4. If you were given a window into heaven to peek through, what would you see?
5. Tell the group about the pets you look forward to seeing in heaven.
6. During Pastor Jorge's brother's funeral, he compared the transition from this life to the next to a sailboat that is out of sight. What do you think about this idea? Can you come up with another way of describing the transition?
7. Jesus spoke of mansions in heaven, big spacious places where we will live forever. What kind of *crib* are you looking forward to having? What will it be like?

PART 5

Yes, Let's Go There

1 0

The Donut Shop Heckler

Positive thinking will let you do everything
better than negative thinking will.

ZIG ZIGLAR[21]

AMONG THE SEVERAL doughnut shops in my town, there are two that
make them incredibly tasty. One advertises with bright neon lights
when their glazed round pieces of *pure heaven* are hot. I can eat one
of those warm scrumptious things in just one bite; not because it's
small, but because it is moist and kind of melts in your mouth when
you stuff it in there.

My brother Hector used to tell me that he could eat a whole doz-
en in one sitting, not because he was depressed, but just because he
could. They are that good. When I see the *Hot Now* sign, my car automatically wants to turn there. It takes sheer inner strength to keep
the steering wheel straight and on the road.

The other local shop offers a great variety of insanely good donuts. They even make weird ones that have fried pieces of bacon on
them. Genius! Everything tastes better with bacon!

This shop also sells a new variety of pastry that has taken the market by storm—a ridiculous combo of a buttery croissant and a sweet donut blended into one delightful treat. Who would have *thunk* it?

Of course we all need to exercise caution with our sugar intake and the foods we eat, but most people's *beef* with donut eating is the false sense of guilt it produces. And donuts are just one of many pleasures society frowns upon. There's pizza, ice cream, chocolate-covered potato chips…the list goes on.

The Image Beast

The focus of our society is so much on the physical that indulging in sweets once in a while plagues the conscience. So we try to play a balancing act of counting calories, saturated fat grams, carbs, sugars, protein, and fiber. We calculate and abstain and exercise, only to take a good look in the mirror and feel totally discouraged. That is why when I order a big burger with fries I order a diet drink with it. It just makes me feel better about myself.

Let's get personal for the next two chapters. The donut shop heckler is the voice that reminds you over and over again of how 'awful' you look. But this evil heckler does not cut you down just because of your weight; it also seeks to defeat you and bring you down by naming everything negative about you, every little imperfection you have. The heckler will try to devalue you by pointing out your curvaceous (or too-thin) body, the cellulite in your legs, your obvious rolls, your pimples, your height or lack thereof, your eyes being too close together or too far apart, and your bushy uni-brow.

Our minds should be our BFFs (Best Friends Forever), but they heckle and exaggerate so we think worse of ourselves.

I hated a picture of myself that Mom loved. The image is very clear in my memory. I am an eight-year-old with a bright smile, holding my two fat chickens, one under each of my arms. Anyone else may think it is a cute shot, but in my mind I look as plump as the birds.

Mom used to say I was just a *husky* kid, but I knew better. In those days I was also shorter than most kids my age and had a squeaky voice. Of course I grew out of that, but deep in my subconscious there is still a fear that I may regress to that stage. Every once in a while I am reminded of that when the voice of a stranger on the phone calls me "Ma'am."

A sporting goods store I visited a few years ago had a sale on spandex biker shorts. I was so excited to try on a pair…NOT! I knew I was in trouble when I walked into a fitting room that had glaring bright lights overhead and three mirrors angled in different directions so I could see all of me. After pulling and grunting, forcing those shorts on, I saw that they revealed all the flubber in my blubber, the jelly in my belly, the junk in my trunk. I thought, *Mankind should never see this*. That day the donut shop heckler discouraged me. It was both ridiculous and heartbreaking.

You (and I) must silence and overcome this vicious heckler in your crowd the moment it attacks your self-esteem.

Our society and media have been shining the spotlight on looks and image for so long, and their influence has been so strong, they are affecting this upcoming generation in a deadly way.

Think about bullying and how it has driven nice individuals to take lives—others' as well as their own. The bully's attacks, based on lies, are simple: "everyone thinks you're fat and ugly" and "no one likes you; no one wants you around" and "do everyone a favor and move away." Those are some mild comments compared to some of the actual writings going on in cyber world. If the recipient of that kind of bullying doesn't have a strong self-esteem, the results can be devastating.

You may not have been cyber-bullied when you were growing up, but you can probably still recall the nicknames other children gave you. As I write this, names like "clutch leg," and "ham bone," immediately pop into my mind. Those two names were related to my scarred left knee and leg. Nicknames are an all-out assault on a person's self-confidence.

You may recall the motorcycle accident I described in chapter seven involving my brother and me. For five years after the accident, I had to wear a huge leg brace to keep the bottom part of my leg working with my knee. The brace went from my upper thigh to a little above my ankle. These days you often see linemen on the football field wearing them. But they were uncommon when I was prescribed one. I became so self-conscious, I asked Mom to buy me extra-wide-legged pants in hopes that no one at the high school I attended would notice my brace.

One day I was sitting in a classroom and a kid came to ask me a question. Inadvertently he hit the thick metal of the brace underneath my pants. He didn't know I had a brace on and it scared him. I felt so weird. I vowed to do all I could never to let anyone know about my leg. The donut shop heckler was messing with my mind big time, even at an early age.

We can be so concerned about what others think of us or what they'll say about us behind our backs. It's debilitating and puts a ceiling to our potential.

Mirror, Mirror

Sometime back I watched an episode of a reality television show, *Total Divas*. One of the main characters was complaining about how out of shape and ugly she was. The truth was that she has a great looking face and an athletic, well-defined body. But she didn't see herself that way. She felt that her image in the mirror was hideous. So her husband and best friend tried to help her by doing an exercise with her.

They took her to a house and asked her to stand-alone in a room facing a mirror. They also hooked her up to a microphone. She had to describe herself to an artist in another room of the house, someone who had never seen her.

As she spoke, the artist drew a sketch based on her description. With sort of a disgusted look on her face she said something like, "Ok, I have long hair, broad shoulders, and I am shaped like a pear. I have fat rolls and big hips and cellulite in the back of my legs." Mind you, this woman had very little body fat anywhere in her body.

After she described her appearance, the artist's partner joined her in the room and described her through the microphone. Again the painter drew a picture strictly based on what he was hearing. His partner's version was completely different from what the woman had said. His description went something like, "She has long hair, her shoulders are proportionate to her body, she has a well-defined body, an hour glass figure…she must be like a size 2…"

When the exercise was over, the woman met the artist in the other room and he presented her with both versions of his sketch. When she saw the pictures, she began to cry because of the marked difference between what she perceived and complained about and the reality of how others saw her.

If you were to describe yourself to someone who has never seen you, what words would you use? Would they be positive or negative, complimentary or sarcastic? And how would you sound while describing yourself: enthusiastic or dull? Being healthy is important, but trying to fit in with society's customs is a mistake

In our culture we are constantly bombarded with images of how the media believes people ought to look. Thin is in, they challenge us! And if you don't look a certain way or fit into a certain dress size, you are marked as ugly and devalued as a person. Of course you and I know that your value as a person is not dependent on public opinion, but hearing so much of the distorted message short circuits our left brain functions so that we start believing that false logic and thus become unhappy with ourselves.

At the Potter's House

Paul wrote to the Christians in Rome, "'But, my friend, I ask, "Who do you think you are to question God? Does the clay have the right to ask the potter why he shaped it the way he did? Doesn't a potter have the right to make a fancy bowl and a plain bowl out of the same lump of clay?"'" (Romans 9:20–21 CEV)

When you and I read that, our eyes automatically gravitate toward that word 'lump.' "I'm one big lump," we complain. "I'm just a plain bowl. Lord, why didn't you make me a fancy one instead? You blew it with me, God."

The opinionated media fashionistas are not alone to blame for our lack of self-confidence. We are a faulted, spiritually fallen humanity, and that influences how we see ourselves as well.

I'm sure you could list a bunch of things in a hurry that you don't like about yourself: "My hair is flat, I'm too short, I'm stupid," and on and on you go. I've heard people with curly hair wishing it was flat and those with flat hair wishing it was curly. Tall people wish they were shorter while short people complain they are not tall enough. Skinny people want to gain a few pounds and those of us with extra poundage want to shed a few.

Remember one thing: God doesn't make mistakes! He formed each of us as we are and loves you and me with all His Being. I find the following Scripture very encouraging, "God does not see the same way people see. People look at the outside of a person, but the LORD looks at the heart" (1Samuel 16:7b NCV).

Take a good look at yourself through God's eyes. When the Lord looks at you (and me), He is not thinking of your waist, shoe, or bra size. He loves you just the way you are. He looks deep into your heart and says, "YES! You are Mine. I love you. I have a great plan for your life. I am going to do amazing things with you and through you—if you let me."

If you ever find yourself complaining about how you look, two very important and dangerous things are happening. One, you are moving in a direction that is completely opposite of what God thinks and wants. Two, you are finding fault with God. Complaining about your imperfections is thinking that He made a mistake when He created you, thinking that God failed! You are having issues with God's wisdom and ways. Anytime you do not view yourself with healthy pride and acceptance, you are discrediting God.

You may read the following and nod, "You made my whole being; you formed me in my mother's body" (Psalm 139:13 NCV). You wholeheartedly agree with that statement, but you may clash with the next verse, "I praise you because you made me in an amazing and wonderful way. What you have done is wonderful. I know this very well" (Psalm 139:14 NCV).

Many people feel like crossing that statement out of their Bibles with a permanent black marker because they do not feel wonderful and amazing. Don't allow the heckler to rob you of the joy and excitement of being you.

To silence the donut shop heckler, you must leave the Potter's house not only believing in the sovereignty and craftsmanship of the Potter, but also celebrating the beauty and worth of what He shaped and molded: You!

Live Out Loud

At the time of this writing Erica Jean is a beautiful young woman who wears clothes size 18. She turned a lot of heads when she first appeared on the front cover of *Women's Running Magazine* in their August, 2015, issue. The response to her appearance in the social media has been incredible and overwhelming. While many women are very insecure about their appearance Erica is an example of someone who accepts herself and feels good about who she is and what she looks like, curves and all.[22]

Brilliant! Now, can anyone with a deeply rooted poor self-concept change his/her outlook? The answer is a resounding "YES." To silence the donut shop heckler, you must recognize that the battleground is your mind. That's the control center for everything you do, and you must take the reins.

Tell your mind where to go. Letting poor thoughts run loose will spell doomsday for you. But when you discipline your mind to be positive and hopeful, everything about you will change.

The wisest man who ever lived, Solomon, wrote that as a person thinks in his/her heart, so he/she is (Proverbs 23:7 NASB).

When your donut shop heckler starts making disturbing remarks, bring it under subjection. Consider the example of longeing.

Longeing is a technique used when training a horse so it can be mounted and ridden. The process is slow and involves repetition and reward. The horse is wild by nature, but the trainer contains the animal inside a round, fenced-in cage and attaches a rope (a longe) to the horse. The trainer then will stand in the middle of the cage holding onto the other end of the rope while the horse walks and trots in circles within the fence. Eventually the horse starts yielding to commands as the trainer gently pulls on the rope, teaching the horse to stop, walk, and trot on command. Repetition, patience, and calmness with the horse are critical. That's just one part of training a horse.

To train your wild mind, *repetition* is paramount. Every day remind yourself out loud, "I am special. I am talented. I am gifted. I have a great future in front of me. God loves me. I will succeed." Repeat that every morning, midday, and evening. And say it out loud so you can hear yourself.

Doreen and I knew an older couple that owned a beautiful home in an area called the Mesa on the outskirts of Taos, New Mexico. To get to their home we had to go off the paved road and onto a dirt road that went up and down through hills. Our friends were active seniors who loved God and life. Munching on raw garlic as if it was candy, they would go up and down those dirt roads repeating out loud, "I am strong. I am special. I am God's child. I am healthy. I am talented. I am gifted. I will succeed." Those two special people taught my bride and me to think positive thoughts.

Please, right now, STOP READING, mark this page, and repeat those statements out loud (it can even be a loud whisper). Adopt those words as your own. Believe in what you are saying! Later, do it again. Every day. Repetition is key to success. Make those statements often enough and you will start believing them. By doing that you are taking a serious step toward silencing the donut shop heckler.

Sometimes people repeat the wrong things to themselves: "I'm not as thin as her." "I'm not as successful as her." "I'm not as good looking as him." It is one question after another: "Why can't I be as funny as him?" "What's wrong with me?" "Why don't I make as much money as other people my age?" "Why don't I have a happy marriage like theirs?" "How come others don't like me as much as they do her?" On and on we go. You must stop the comparison game long enough to recognize your uniqueness. You are indeed special!

Have you ever stopped to consider that maybe, just maybe, those people you are comparing yourself to struggle like everyone else—that they may be wishing they were like you?

The donut shop heckler within you is out to get you. Everything about you is fair game. Silence it!

Replace your negative thoughts with completely opposite ones. Fight it one negative thought, one negative statement at a time. Ask the Lord to reconfigure your mind so you can see yourself from His point of view. Take charge! Believe something good and positive is coming your way. It's the way to overcome. And maybe, just maybe, pop a clove of garlic in your mouth… just for the fun of it!

What's Your Take?

1. When it comes to food, what is your greatest weakness? Is it a certain kind of dessert or type of food?
2. The old saying goes, "Sticks and stones may break my bones but words will never hurt me." Is that statement true or false? Explain your answer.
3. The Bible describes God as a potter working at the wheel, shaping and molding our lives. Can you think of God as a mechanic? Why? How is the Lord like a counselor? Compare God to a master chef.
4. It's a curious thing that we have reversed the way God operates. He disregards what we look like on the outside and is mainly concerned with our inside. When God looks inside your heart, what positive qualities does He see? Name a few of the great traits that make you, you!
5. Why is the comparison game not a fair game to play?
6. Positive reinforcement and repetition are significant parts of bringing our minds under God's control. The Bible helps us reform our minds, and the Church can reinforce God's view of us. What could you do to help others defeat the Donut Shop Heckler?

1 1

The Heckler of Failure

Success is stumbling from failure to
failure with no loss of enthusiasm.

WINSTON S. CHURCHILL[23]

IT WAS THE sixth game of the 2012 Stanley Cup finals between the
LA Kings and the New Jersey Devils. The Kings were up three games
to two with the sixth game being played in Los Angeles. It was an
intense game. The crowd roared with every hit and every shot on goal.
Then something happened that determined the outcome of the game.

With adrenalin pumping off the charts, Steve Bernier (one of the
Devil's players) violently smashed King's player Rob Scuderi's head
against the board, sending him to the ice bleeding. Bernier was eject-
ed from the game for failing to play by the rules and committing
an infraction called *Boarding*. Because of his actions, the Kings were
given a five-minute power play.

During a power play one team has at least a one-person advantage
over the other. During the next five minutes of play the Kings took
advantage of their player advantage and scored three goals in a row,
enough to give them their first Stanley Cup Championship.

Failure happens! Not just in sports, but in life! A few flops of my
own come to mind:

- I forgot my date's name in the middle of our date and she had to remind me what it was. Needless to say she never went out with me again. A similar bungle happened after I had been married a few weeks. I failed to remember my bride's name when introducing her to one of my professors at seminary… YIKES…I'm glad to report that she forgave me for that hideous blunder and we have been happily married now for over 30 years.
- I was subjected to a lie detector test for work at a bank. After a battery of questions they quickly showed me the way out.
- I failed to pass my Florida teacher's certification exam after graduating from college with a bachelor's degree in foreign language education.
- I once attempted to replace the timing chain in my car. After dropping half the engine, installing the new chain, and putting the whole thing back together again, the car did not start. I had botched the job! The good news is that I learned where I had made a mistake, took half the engine apart once again, and fixed it so the car chirped like a bird and ran like a champ.

Those are just a few failures that quickly popped into my mind. There are plenty more where those came from, and there will be plenty more in the future.

If you're like most people, your failures tend to stick out in your mind more than your achievements. We are all guilty of replaying over and over in our minds the scenes of times we came short of the expected goal.

Good parents of rebellious children often punish themselves with false guilt, thinking they must have failed as a parent for their kids to turn out as they have. Former partners of a failed marriage also cannot seem to get over what each did wrong to cause the breakup. Failure re-runs are just awful, especially if you have a hard time forgiving yourself. Living with a mind full of regret and guilt is not living at all.

Loser... Who, Me?

One way to silence the heckler of failure is not to dwell on it for long.

Sometimes I get discouraged—and a few times downright depressed—about my lack of achievements and my past failures. Unfortunately, when I'm down, I drag everyone else down with me. Those who know me well choose to stay far from me when they sense I'm on my way down.

I once asked a very successful older preacher I looked up to if he ever got depressed in ministry. His answer was quick and decisive. With his booming voice he answered, "George…yes, I do, but I never let it go for long." I never forgot that.

Stop entertaining thoughts about your shortcomings that make you feel like a loser.

God never intended for you to get depressed or feel like a loser because of the mistakes you have made or because of how things have turned out in your life. He prewired you (and all humans) with a spirit of resilience. His Spirit will help you look beyond your failure, adapt, and bounce back.

I have heard it said that failure is a detour, not a dead-end street. Our "mess-ups" are just bumps on the road. Don't let your failure trip you up and keep you down on your journey to success.

Have you gotten frustrated driving behind a slow car in the fast lane of the highway? So you shift gears and change lanes quickly, only to find that a few feet later your lane comes to a complete stop while the cars in the lane you left continue moving pass you. If you are an impatient driver steam will be oozing out of your ears.

In your success journey, patience is critical. Accept failure as a part of your life. Expect it! Don't aim for it, but expect it.

It reminds me of little Jimmy learning to ride a bike. His dad took him to an empty parking lot without parking stops but with one light post in the middle. Just before Jimmy launched into his first solo trip he asked, "What about that light over there?" The dad answered, "What about it, what do you mean?" Jimmy responded, "What if I hit it?" Dad said, "Don't think about that light post, Jimmy. Look at all the area you have to ride your bike around. Just stay away from it. You'll be ok!" But the moment Jimmy took off he started heading straight towards the light post. He yelled, "Daddy...daddy...I'm going to the light, I'm going to the light!" Dad yelled back, "Don't look at it. Don't focus on it. Go the other way. Turn the wheel, Son." But Jimmy could not get the post out of his sight and, sure enough, crashed into it.

Never think you are going to fail at anything. Dream big and give it your best shot, but be real with yourself and know that even if you fail, you can always try again.

Botched Lives

It is comforting to know that our Bible ancestors have been making mistakes and failing as far back as the Garden of Eden. You and I mess up because we are sin-prone, imperfect humans living in a cursed world. Look at how some of our heroes of the faith botched their lives:

David, the man after God's own heart, failed God by lusting and committing adultery with a married woman. He also mercilessly killed her husband to cover up his indiscretion (2Samuel 11:1-24 NIV).

Peter failed the Lord by denying knowing Him three times, cursing to His face, and leaving Jesus to face the wrath of the Romans alone (Luke 22:54-62 NIV).

Samson (an Old Testament type of *Hulk*) failed to keep the secret of his supernatural strength from Delilah (a girl working in a covert operation for Samson's enemies). As a result, Samson eventually lost his life (Judges 16:17-31).

King Zedekiah failed to listen to Jeremiah's warning and advice about a Babylonian invasion and how to handle it. When the Babylonians came, Zedekiah was forced to watch his sons being slaughtered. Afterward they gouged out his eyes, put him in chains, and led him away (2Kings 25:1-7).

Mark, one of Paul's companions in missions, quit while in the middle of a missionary journey and missed out on an adventure of a lifetime (Acts 13:13).

As sad as those real-life episodes may be, it is refreshing to know that we are not alone when we fail. Be certain that your feelings of inadequacy (and mine) have plagued others before you. You're on a trail that others have trodden upon long before you got there. You just have to keep trying and trying and trying, even if (and when) you fail again and again and again.

Ultimate victory comes through failure!

The Belmont Stakes is the third leg of horseracing's biggest stage, the Triple Crown. A three-year-old colt named Palace Malice won the Belmont Stakes in 2013. The big deal is that Palace Malice had won only one of his last seven races and took twelfth place in a field of twenty horses in the first leg of the Triple Crown, the Kentucky Derby. Palace Malice won the Belmont Stakes by beating Orb, the winner of the Kentucky Derby, and Oxbow, the winner of the Preakness, the Triple Crown's second race. Palace Malice had failed many times but his owners believed they had a winner in Palace Malice. They were right!

Do you see yourself as a winner despite past failures? God does!

You are going to mess up along the way. But don't let the heckler of failure put you down and make you feel like you have no future. Hecklers in your crowd will hold you back. Silence them by continuing to try.

I have a friend who is a very successful businesswoman and philanthropist. But to get there she had to overcome a very difficult life. When her husband became abusive she had to run away and found herself with nothing but her young children and her God. But instead of giving in to discouragement she became determined to succeed. And through years of faith, hard work, and courage she conquered one problem after another. She was not only able to provide for her children but she also established safe homes for women who find themselves in need of protection and hope.

Turning Negatives Into Positives

Stop! Change! Determine from now on to see failure from a different perspective. Turn what seems like a bad thing into a good thing. Let it be your motivator to do better. Think of a child learning to walk. She will take one step and fall right on her boom-boom. Then she'll get up, try again, lose her balance and fall back on her diaper. That child hasn't learned the word *fail* yet. All she knows is that walking looks like lots of fun. So the child will try again and again until walking becomes her way of moving about. But not for long; once she's figured out how to stay upright and walk, running and climbing becomes her norm.

If past failures have knocked you down, get up and run. Do it! Be determined. Settle for nothing less.

I realize that failing doesn't feel good at the time; it bruises and hurts our egos. Trust me. I've been there many times. But in the grand scheme of things, and if hindsight is 20/20, as you look back at your life you will realize something good came out of an experience you thought was bad. Instead of waiting for later to realize that failure can be a good thing, why not look at it that way while you are failing?

Remember the young missionary, Mark? He left Paul while they were in the middle of an assignment. He failed! The Bible tells us that Paul got so mad about it that he parted ways with both Mark and Barnabas, Paul's partner, who wanted to take Mark on another trip. Mark later made a huge turnaround and became instrumental in the work of God. Years later, near the end of his life, the apostle Paul wrote, "Only Luke is with me. Get Mark and bring him with you, because he is helpful to me in my ministry" (2Timothy 4:11 NIV).

Obviously Mark had come to the crossroads of realizing his actions and how he had failed. He then took whatever steps were necessary to get back on a successful ministry path.

David Ramsey wrote that if you want to do well in life you have to learn from the mistakes you make along the way.[24]

Maybe while you're reading this you also find yourself at a crossroads. You may have made a costly mistake in your past, but your next step is critical if you want to move forward.

You can drop your head and drag your feet around while kicking cans along the way, or you can learn from what happened, get a new vision for your life, pick yourself back up, and move ahead. Refusing to quit after you've failed is absolutely essential in defeating this nasty heckler of failure.

Jonah was an Old Testament prophet who failed to obey when God told him to go preach in a city called Nineveh. The Bible says, "The word of the Lord came to Jonah son of Amittai: 'Go to the great city of Niniveh and preach against it, because its wickedness has come up before me.' But Jonah ran away from the Lord and headed for Tarshish" (Jonah 1:1-3a NIV).

Tarshish was in the opposite direction of Nineveh, where God was pointing, and Jonah boarded a ship to go there. Have you refused to listen to the voice of God in your heart?

On the way a furious storm broke out. After a while, the sailors figured out that God was after Jonah so they "heave-hoed" the prophet overboard. Then God sent a great big fish to swallow Jonah alive. While Jonah was slish-sloshing in gastric juices, he repented of his failure. The fish swam close to shore and, at God's command, vomited Jonah out by the beach.

Picture Jonah, if you will, smelling pretty ripe, slimy junk hanging off him, seaweed in his hair. Jonah was weak, dehydrated, sleep deprived, and in need of nourishment.

"Then the word of the LORD came to Jonah a second time: 'Go to the great city of Nineveh and proclaim to it the message I give you.' Jonah obeyed the word of the LORD and went to Nineveh" (Jonah 3:1–3a NIV). Jonah dusted the sticky sand off of him and did what God wanted.

God is a second chance God! He will make sure new opportunities emerge after you have failed. Put your failures behind you and move forward. Never quit trying!

I heard John Maxwell say at a conference that Michael Michalko studied and wrote about Thomas Edison's creativity and work. He wrote that Edison conducted over 50,000 experiments before perfecting the alkaline storage cell battery.[25] Can you imagine trying fifty thousand times?

In his book *Something to Smile About,* Zig Ziglar tells about the Ford Motor Company designing the Edsel many years ago and how it turned out to be a horrible failure. Consumers were not buying it. Ford lost millions of dollars. But the automotive engineers kept thinking and working towards producing a great product. Eventually the Mustang was introduced to the public and later the Taurus. Both became huge successes.[26]

One more example of refusing to quit is the sixteenth president of the United States of America, Abraham Lincoln. His failures over the span of many years have been well documented. He lost a job, had a nervous breakdown, failed in business, and was defeated for public office not once or twice or even three times but seven times. And after all of that, Lincoln became president. Can you imagine?

Don't give up. Refuse to quit. Even when you do not feel like it, say to yourself: "I'm not going to let this keep me down. I'm going to fight through it and go on!"

One of the dangers of failure is that it may rob you of future success, if you allow it to.

Maybe young Mark, the missionary, left the ministry for a while because he was afraid of not having what it took to be like Paul and his companions.

Moses was afraid of being unqualified for the job of leading God's people out of Egypt. That is why he argued with God and gave Him all kinds of excuses for not wanting to go when the Lord called him to rescue His people from Pharaoh (Exodus 3).

Fear of the known and the unknown can paralyze you and hold you back from realizing your goals and dreams. Careful, the truth is that most people's fears are never realized.

I was so excited about the prospect of graduating from Seminary and receiving a Master's Degree. My mom had promised she would be there to celebrate the occasion with me. But as the graduation time drew near mom became more and more adamant about being there. I was living in New Orleans at the time and she resided in Orlando, Florida. She feared her plane would crash in the waters of the Gulf of Mexico so she didn't make it to my big day. Her fear held her back.

I had not led Vacation Bible School for children (VBS) for many years. Then years ago, out of necessity, I had to take the reins. I was petrified. VBS was to start on a Monday morning, and Sunday night I was a wreck at home. My darling wife sat me down, and in a way I understood it explained how I could lead VBS. Her counsel made all the difference in the world!

Monday morning came and I was sweating bullets, but the week ran smoothly. All the credit goes to the volunteers who made it happen. They were the reason for our success. But if I had given in to my fears and failed to lead, I would never have enjoyed the fruit of seeing kids have a blast as they learned about Jesus. We also had the joy of seeing some of them give their lives to Jesus Christ as Savior.

You are going to fail along the way, but don't let the emotional damage be permanent. Good can come out of bad. Positive follows negative. Favorable outcomes emerge from unfavorable circumstances. Don't let the heckler of failure take you down for the count. Stand up to it. Fight back your fear. In time you will enjoy the fruit of success!

All of this is doable! Let God, your Creator, the One who loves you and knows you best, tweak you from the inside out. And know that the God who leads you equips you. He specializes in getting people from failure to success.

Are you stalled out? Maybe what you were doing stopped working and left you frustrated. God is an expert at tinkering with peoples' messes. Go to Him. Talk with Him. Let the Lord Jesus jump-start your life. Quit feeling guilty and sorry for the inevitable failures in life and bounce back, refusing to get discouraged; you will overcome!

A friend of mine made some mistakes that led him to prison. He stayed there for a long time. Then, one day, he knocked at my door. At first I didn't recognize him as he just stood there silently. Then it hit me. My friend had been transformed while being incarcerated.

He had asked Jesus Christ in his heart and had begun taking a series of steps towards moving forward in life. He received education in jail that would secure him a job when he was released. He took advantage of medical and health related incentive the prison system offers. He exercised daily. In other words, he grew spiritually, mentally, and physically.

He said: "I noticed several other inmates did nothing with their lives while serving their prison sentences. Hour after hour, day after day, week after week would pass by while they did nothing with their lives. I decided to be different and here I am today." Today my friend is doing great, has steady work, and continues to push forward through life.

What holds you back? What is that one thing that you feel is insurmountable? Remember Paul's words, "For I can do everything through Christ, who gives me strength" (Philippians 4:13).

What's Your Take?

1. Reread the quote by Winston Churchill, "Success is stumbling from failure to failure with no loss of enthusiasm." When you set out to do something, what do you find discourages you most?

2. Pastor Jorge named some of his most memorable flops. Name one of your most memorable failures. When do you think you dropped the ball?

3. Our failures seem to stand out in our minds more than our successes; they stick to us like glue. What do you think is the best formula for forgiving yourself?

4. The author mentions false guilt that parents sometimes carry on their shoulders because of how their children turn out. Is that sense of failure justified? How would you define false guilt? Can children of great parents become messed-up adults? Why or why not?

5. In the story of little Jimmy crashing into a pole in the parking lot, can you identify with him? Have there been times in your life when you focused on the wrong thing? What is the best way to refocus?

6. How does it make you feel to know that great Bible characters struggled as you do? Can you identify with a favorite struggling Bible character?

7. Pastor Jorge writes: "God is a second-chance God!" Describe a time when you feel you received a second chance. This could be at work, in sports, in a relationship, etc. How does the Lord give us a second chance at life and eternity?

1 2

Let the Disruption End!

By prevailing over all obstacles and
distractions, one may unfailingly arrive
at his chosen goal or destination.

CHRISTOPHER COLUMBUS[27]

As WE WRAP up these ideas of overcoming the hecklers in our crowd, let's clear the air on hecklers. Some are selfish individuals who pursue their own agenda regardless of how it may affect others. Hecklers can be sneaky or out in the open. They may be obnoxiously loud or quiet as a whisper. Their poison can set you back for a short time or for a lifetime. Hecklers come from every direction, for any reason, and usually when you least expect it (unless you are able to see them coming).

Other hecklers are seemingly insurmountable circumstances that shake you emotionally and psychologically. Difficulties have a way of making us doubt our talents and abilities, even our worth as a person. And then when we are down it becomes easy for us to question God's love and plan for our lives—like the person who said to me, "No offense, preacher, but I don't think God even cares about my situation."

The truth is that God never forgets His own. He knows your name, your address, and what you are going through. In fact, the Lord is like a sentry, never taking His loving eyes off you! (Psalm 121:4).

Throughout the book I have shared some specific, relevant ideas and concepts on how to silence and overcome the negative voices in your life. There are also three principles to live by that will help you overcome hecklers on a day-to-day basis: the PCTs (Pace, Control, Time).

Three Daily Amigos

1. Pace! Commit yourself to resolving matters quickly. We often tend to make things bigger and far worse than they appear.

Recently my daughter and I were going out the door of our home. When she walked through the doorframe, she shrieked and ran all the way to the middle of the road. There was a snake sunning itself against the wall of the house on our front porch. It was a black snake, what I call a *good* snake. They eat mice and rats and pests you don't want on your property. It wasn't a venomous serpent but a nice one, a rather large nice one; nonetheless, it caught my daughter by surprise.

All Sara had to do was walk away from it. Instead she bolted in terror. I simply stayed inside the house and locked the door, leaving Sara outside. We were laughing so hard (me inside and she in the middle of the street) because there was no real reason for panic.

People and problems can be like that snake. They may appear worse than they really are, making you anxious and stressed out. Some people get physically ill over nothing but annoying hecklers in their crowd. Allowing hecklers to keep bothering you can make you the proud parent of a baby ulcer.

Settle matters quickly and wisely.

Instead of playing ostrich by burying your head in the sand and hoping it all goes away, tackle your heckler with God's help. Ask Him to intervene on your behalf and remove the thorn in your flesh and the pain in your neck.

An English idiom says, "Nip it in the bud." The Bible's counterpart is, "The end of a matter is better than its beginning" (Ecclesiastes 7:8a NIV). In other words, try to deal with a difficult matter in its early stages before it has the potential of becoming a greater problem for you.

I met a man years ago who had lost touch with his brother. They had not communicated for many years. I scratched the surface of that subject a little and he told me that he and his brother had been close when they were growing up. So I asked what happened. He told me that there had been a strong disagreement between the two of them and they stopped talking. The man was not even sure of his brother's whereabouts at the time. I said something like, "Man, your fight must have been over something really important." The man's answer stunned me. He said, "To tell you the truth I don't even remember what it was all about."

Why do we let problems fester? Try to resolve matters quickly. Life is too short and precious to be wasted on trivial matters.

The apostle Paul wrote, "In your anger do not sin: Do not let the sun go down while you are still angry, and do not give the devil a foothold" (Ephesians 4:26–27 NIV).

Let me paint a picture for you. Imagine wanting a bad situation to be over. You want to shut the door on that heckler, hoping to never deal with that situation again. But when you push to slam the door shut, the devil sticks his foot between the door and the doorframe so it can remain open, allowing the problem to continue festering. That is the image of giving the devil a foothold.

Paul was urging us not to let angry feelings simmer and boil in us overnight. When left unchecked, our minds will magnify things and blow them out of proportion, thus allowing the enemy to stir things up worse.

God's wisdom tells us to keep unpleasant situations short. Resolve matters quickly!

One more idea about pacing, spend time on those things and people that are really important. I remember reading a little booklet years ago called *The Tyranny of the Urgent*. What I got out of that writing is that urgent situations in life tend to manipulate our time and effort. As a result, we forsake what's genuinely important for the sake of those things that we think we must do right away.

This idea became real to me one day several years ago when I was asked to go to the hospital because one of our members was in route there in an ambulance. I was in the middle of something very important but I dropped everything and headed that way. When I reached the emergency room I identified myself and asked to see the certain individual that should have already been there. But the person couldn't be found. After the volunteer made a thorough search for that person I was told that no one had arrived in an ambulance and that such person was not registered anywhere in the hospital record.

I went back to my car wondering about it all and after making a few phone calls I found out the person had not been in an ambulance or even gone to the hospital. Someone had gotten the story wrong and given me false information. It was an honest mistake but the seemingly urgent matter had interrupted something essential that I was doing and robbed me of a couple of hours of my time.

Never allow people or circumstances to determine your agenda. Pace yourself! Prioritize!

2. Control! Keep your mind under control at all times—God's control!

Regardless of where you find yourself today, whether at peace or dealing with hecklers, I challenge you to memorize this short statement from the apostle Paul: "We take captive every thought to make it obedient to Christ" (2Corinthians 10:5 NIV).

When you internalize that verse, the Spirit of God has a way of bringing it to mind when you most need it. That one Scripture has helped me many times. If you are anything like me, your mind can become your best ally or your worst enemy.

Let God be in charge of what you are thinking. That is not an easy task, but it is a necessary discipline. The mind, as the Lord made it, is like a supercomputer analyzing data that comes in through the various senses at every moment. This data can be both good and bad.

The mind is a powerful instrument that must be kept in check at all times. For example, have you ever been in church when some random, ugly, evil thought pops into your mind? You catch yourself and think, *What in the world? Where did that come from?* You did not do anything to provoke that thought, it just happened.

Thoughts happen!

Your choice is to entertain that thought—mull it over—or take control of it. Pray, "Lord, this thought is not from you. I take this thought captive and make it obedient to Jesus Christ." At that point, the Holy Spirit takes over and helps you overcome.

It is vital for God to be in control of your mind, not only to overcome the hecklers in your crowd, but also to just live life in general. The Holy Spirit in you is an expert at turning a negative thought around.

I have heard it said that where Messiah is there is no misery. We like to believe that. The problem is that when miserable times happen we begin to wonder, *Where was God when that mess was going on?* Or, *How come the Lord didn't intervene when it all got bad for me?* That may be the human way of responding to tough times, but it is not healthy thinking.

When you let God control your mind, when you are focusing on His will, His purposes for you, and His grace and love, His Holy Spirit gives you a new perspective. The phrase, "Where Messiah is there is no misery" will change to "Where there is misery there is Messiah!" That shift in thinking results in God lifting a huge weight off our shoulders. That is how the Lord works. It is how He rolls.

Let God's Spirit shape and mold your mind by allowing Him to be in control of it. Reflect on Him daily and often (Colossians 3:2). The Lord is an overcoming Genius!

3. Time! Treat it as a friend and don't let it become a foe.

Time is precious and yet it is so easy to waste.

We are such an up-tempo society. We love to expedite and ship overnight. If you are like me, you hate red lights and slow fast food drive-through. I say to myself, *Good help is so hard to find* when transactions do not happen fast. After all, I have places to go, people to see, things to do...but really? That is just what we say to justify our rude behavior.

People say, "I can't help it; I am a product of my environment." However, the Lord Jesus within you wants you to refuse that kind of thinking and become a product of His kingdom. Wise King Solomon wrote: "There is a time for everything, and a season for every activity under the heavens: a time to be born and a time to die, a time to plant and a time to uproot, a time to kill and a time to heal, a time to tear down and a time to build, a time to weep and a time to laugh, a time to mourn and a time to dance, a time to scatter stones and a time to gather them, a time to embrace and a time to refrain from embracing, a time to search and a time to give up, a time to keep and a time to throw away, a time to tear and a time to mend, a time to be silent and a time to speak, a time to love and a time to hate, a time for war and a time for peace" (Ecclesiastes 3:1–8 NIV).

Time is man's friend! You have 24 hours, 1,440 minutes, 86,400 seconds every day to make things happen. If you live 77 years, you will have 676,800 hours available to you. And that, sometimes it seems, is not enough. Take advantage of every opportunity before you!

Charles Darwin once said, "A man who dares to waste one hour of life has not discovered the value of life."

Use your time wisely! What are you passionate about? Do those things. Keep spending time with the people you love. Life is too short to be wasted worrying about hecklers and all the what-ifs associated with them. Determine that today is your chance to start overcoming and moving forward.

Time is critical for maintaining sanity and excitement in life. It is so easy, however, for us to squander minutes and hours on nothing. Just recently I blew off a chunk of precious time for being disorganized.

Sometime back my car had to spend a couple of days at an auto body shop because the antilock braking system needed to be fixed. After I dropped it off, a young man from a car rental company a few miles away picked me up and drove me to their office branch so I could rent a car to drive while my car was being worked on. Once inside the car rental place the young man asked if I had my driver's license with me. Immediately I realized I had left my wallet in my car.

I apologized for the inconvenience and asked the young man to drive me back to the mechanic's shop to get my license. Just before we got there I said, "I'm sorry, you know what, my wallet is not in my car but at my house. Do you mind driving me there? I apologize." The young man was very professional and didn't object, so we detoured and headed to my house a few miles in the other direction. We got to my house and he waited with the engine running while I ran inside my home. I looked on the dining room table, my bedroom, and the bathroom, but couldn't find my wallet anywhere. That's when I realized my wallet was in my car as I had originally thought. I got back in the man's car and said, "I'm so sorry to be wasting your time. Can you drive us to the mechanic shop? My wallet must be in the car." And it was. Ridiculous!

Jesus Knew

Jesus Christ was not a time waster. He lived very conscious of time and managed it perfectly! This is evident even at the very beginning of His ministry when Jesus went to a wedding reception.

It may surprise many believers today that the Lord enjoyed having a good time at a party. People who think Christianity is boring are just ignorant about the Son of God.

Jesus Christ loved life, people, and good times, but at the same time He was laser-beam focused on His purpose and mission on earth. Check out what happened at the wedding reception, "The wine supply ran out during the festivities, so Jesus's mother told him, "They have no more wine." "Dear woman, that's not our problem," Jesus replied. "My time has not yet come" (John 2:3–4).

Running out of wine would have been an absolute disaster and embarrassment for the young couple. So Mary took it upon herself to tell Jesus about the shortage because He had the power to help out. However, the Lord felt it was not the proper time for Him to make a grand miracle that would wow the crowd and manifest His Lordship.

The fascinating thing is that Jesus went ahead and helped anyway. He performed His first miracle by transforming the water into wine, but He did it without any hoopla. Jesus did not want to draw attention to himself.

The Son of God was very methodical in His use of time on earth. He lived under the control of His heavenly Father's will. He said, "For I have come down from heaven not to do my will but to do the will of him who sent me" (John 6:38 NIV).

Your challenge is to live according to God's divine time zone for your life!

My family and I love to go on cruises. Sometimes while on a cruise we visit places that are in a different time zone than from the place where we set sail. So we are constantly reminded to keep our watches set to the ship's time and not to the time zone of the country we are visiting to avoid the risk of returning late to the ship. I am sure there would be a certain nauseating, empty, sad feeling in seeing the ship sail away without us.

Make sure you stay on God's time. Like David, say to yourself and to God, "My times are in your hands" (Psalm 31:15a NIV).

Allow God to monopolize your agenda.

One time Jesus's earthly half-brothers were pushing Him to go to the temple in Jerusalem and show the world the miracles He could do. But He was not in the habit of doing what others wanted. "Jesus said to his brothers, 'The right time for me has not yet come, but any time is right for you'" (John 7:6 NCV).

In other words, they could come and go and do whatever they wanted because they were not being led as Jesus was. The Lord was following a goal, the redemption of mankind by way of the cross. That's why Jesus invaded our world: to save it. He was keenly aware of the value of time. "Before the Passover celebration, Jesus knew that his hour had come to leave this world and return to his Father" (John 13:1a).

While on the cross, "Jesus knew that his mission was now finished, and to fulfill Scripture he said, 'I am thirsty.' A jar of sour wine was sitting there, so they soaked a sponge in it, put it on a hyssop branch, and held it up to his lips. When Jesus had tasted it, he said, 'It is finished!' Then he bowed his head and gave up his spirit" (John 19:28–30). That statement was the exclamation point of a life well managed!

The Lord had many hecklers in His crowd, especially religious ones, but He overcame every one of them and accomplished His life's mission in only thirty-three and a half years! Wow!

Treat time as a friend and, even when a heckler appears, make sure to stay on track.

Above All

One more thing before I wrap this up. You may have a lot going on for you right now, but without Jesus Christ as your Savior and in control of your life, you are missing on the most important aspect of living.

Consider the old story of the guy who bought a talking parrot from the pet store. A few days went by and the guy went back to the pet shop and complained. "That parrot never talks." The parrot expert asked, "Did you buy him the stairs for his cage? He loves the stairs and will talk because he's happy." So the man bought the tiny stairs. A few days later the man returned. "That parrot's still not saying a word." The man at the store asked, "Did you buy him the mirror? He loves to look at himself in the mirror and talk." So the man bought the mirror.

A few days later the man went back with the same complaint. "This is ridiculous," he argued, "I paid a lot of money for that talking parrot and he has yet to say anything." The store clerk asked, "Well, I don't know what to tell you. Did you buy him a swing?" When the man got home with the swing, he found the parrot lying on his back with his legs sticking up in the air. Just before he died, the parrot uttered his first and last words, "Hey, do they sell any bird food at that store you go to?"

Jesus Christ is like high protein food for life. I challenge you to give your life to him. Through Jesus you are able to overcome any heckler that tries to slow you down.

With the Lord in your heart, you gain a new, healthy self-image as you begin to see yourself through the eyes of the One who designed every detail of your being. You gain a new excitement about your life as God meets your insatiable need to be loved unconditionally.

Also, as you discover that the Lord has put together a master plan for your life that was written before you were even born (Psalm 139:15–16), there is anticipation in you of what's next for you.

You develop a new confidence about you since you know that God favors and blesses His followers. Even when life becomes difficult, His Holy Spirit in you helps you persevere and rejoice deep inside, even when there is nothing to smile about.

Chuck Colson told the story of his friend Dois Rosser going to India to help build a church. While there a friend of Dois asked him to go with him to a remote village. They drove for hours until they arrived. It was a small community. When the people came out to greet Dois and his friend he noticed that they were at a colony of lepers. Men, women, and children had limbs missing. Leprosy had disfigured the faces of some. It was quite a sight, but then the people began to sing and they led Dois and his friend to the village's church.

Their place of worship was made of waist high granite rocks assembled and mortared in the shape of a rectangle. The villagers had gotten it all done through begging and would continue doing so until the building was completed (which Dois helped them accomplish in a later trip).

Before Dois and his friend left, the villagers asked if they could pray together. Then, the lepers laid flat on the hot dirt and offered up prayers of thanksgiving to God and praised Him for His loving kindness.[28]

What would make people living in poverty in a terribly desolate place, suffering from a devastating illness be joyous, thankful, and feeling blessed? How could they overcome such hecklers? The answer is Jesus Christ! With Him you are more than a conqueror (Romans 8:37)! Through Him you overcome!

End Notes

1. Ann Graham Lotz, *The Magnificent Obsession: Embracing the God Filled Life* (Grand Rapids, Mich.: Zondervan, 2009), 80-81.

2. Charles Colson, *Against The Night: Living in the New Age Dark Ages* (Ann Arbor, Mich.: Servant Books, 1989), 160.

3. Christ Pleasance, *"Metal detector takes just two HOURS to find gold wedding ring that slipped off pensioner's finger 55 YEARS ago"*, 21 January 2014, http://www.dailymail.co.uk/news/article-2543181/Metal-detector-takes-just-two-HOURS-gold-wedding-ring-slipped-pensioners-finger-55-YEARS-ago.html (Accessed August 5, 2015)

4. Leonard Ravenhill, https://www.goodreads.com/author/quotes/159020.Leonard_Ravenhill (Accessed March 28, 2016)

5. *The Intimidator 305,* Travel Channel Video, http://www.travelchannel.com/shows/insane-coaster-wars-world-domination/video/the-intimidator-305 (Accessed August 5, 2015)

6. Phil Black, Don Melvin, and Ralph Ellis, *CNN, 10 April 2015, 'Heist Investigation: London police didn't respond to burglar alarm'*, http://www.cnn.com/2015/04/10/europe/london-hatton-garden-heist/ (Accessed August 5, 2015)

7. Brainy Quote Quotes, http://www.brainyquote.com/quotes/quotes/h/helenkelle383771.html (Accessed March 28, 2016)

8. Robert Dale, *To Dream Again: How to Help Your Church come Alive*, (Nashville: Broadman Press, 1981), 12.

9. Dave Ramsey, *EntreLeadership: 20 years of Practical Business Wisdom from the Trenches*, (New York: Howard Books, 2011), 23.

10. Dr. David Jeremiah, *'The Coming Economic Earthquake: What Bible Prophecy Warns about the New Global Economy'* (New York: FaithWords, 2010), 239.

11. Ravi Zacharias, *Recapture the Wonder* (Nashville, Tennessee: Thomas Nelson, 2003), 155.

12. *B10NUMB3RS: The Database Of Useful Biological Numbers,* http://bionumbers.hms.harvard.edu/bionumber.aspx?&id=101509 (Accessed August 17, 2015)

13. Ed Young, *Been There. Done that. Now what? The Meaning of Life May Surprise You* (Nashville, Tennessee: Broadman & Holman Publishers), 189.

14. Dave Ramsey, *EntreLeadership: 20 years of Practical Business Wisdom from the Trenches*, (New York: Howard Books, 2011), 119.

15. Sujan Patel, *Success Can Come at Any Age. Just Look at These 6 Successful Entrepreneurs,* https://www.entrepreneur.com/article/241346, (Accessed October 11, 2016)

16. Ibid.

17. Pierce Morgan Live, *Sharks and Reptiles,* Aired 2 August 2013, http://edition.cnn.com/TRANSCRIPTS/1308/02/pmt.01.html (Accessed July 10, 2015)

18. Chuck R. Swindoll, *Strengthening Your Grip: Essentials in an Aimless World* (Waco, Texas: Word Books, 1982), 140.

19. Philippians 1:21, NIV

20. Randy Alcorn, *Heaven* (Wheaton, Illinois: Tyndale House Publishers, 2004), 387.

21. Brainy Quotes, http://www.brainyquote.com/quotes/quotes/z/zigziglar125675.html (Accessed March 29, 2016)

22. Holly Passalaqua, *Plus Sized Model Erica Jean Schenk "Stunned" by Women's Running Cover: I Can Feel The Masses Begging For More,* Thursday July 16, 2015 7:49 pm PDT, http://www.eonline.com/news/677212/plus-sized-model-eric-jean-stunned-by-womens-running-magazine-cover-i-can-feel-the-masses-begging-for-more (Accessed 18 August, 2015)

23. Ekaterina Walter, *Forbes/Entrepreneurs: 30 Powerful Quotes on Failure,* http://www.forbes.com/sites/ekaterinawalter/2013/12/30/30-powerful-quotes-on-failure/#46a2e0fa15d3

24. Dave Ramsey, *Entreleadership: 20 Years of Practical Business Wisdom from the Trenches* (New York, NY: Howard Books, 2011), 5.

25. John Maxwell, '*A Day About Books Conference*', (Writing Lecture, June 23rd, 2012)

26. Zig Ziglar, *Something to Smile About: Encouragement and Inspiration for Life's Ups and Downs* (Nashville, Tennessee: Thomas Nelson, 1997), 187.

27. Wisdom-of-the-Wise.com, Christopher Columbus Quotes, http://www.wisdom-of-the-wise.com/Christopher-Columbus.htm (Accessed March 31, 2016)

28. Charles Colson with Ellen Santilli Vaughn, *The Body: Being Light In Darkness* (Dallas, Texas: Word Publishing, 1992) 138-139.

Scripture Index

2Samuel

5:20	35
11:1-24	146
12:3	121
12:22-23	119

1Kings

19:11-13	78

2Kings

25:1-7	147

1Chronicles

12:6	96

2Chronicles

20:12,15	37

Psalms

5:3	100
10:15	70
30:5	12
31:15	163
33:17	38
34:17-19	93

Proverbs

Ecclesiastes

3:1-8	161
7:8	157

Isaiah

11:6-9	121
43:1-3	61
65: 25	122

Jeremiah

1:5	96
29:11	26
31:3,4,13,14,17	59-60, 70

Jonah

1:1-3	150
3:1-3	150

Matthew

5:44	71
6:34	49
6:27, 34	110
16:21-23	24
19:26	23
28:19-20	6
28:20	62

Mark

10:27	120
9:2-6	124

Luke

1:18	113
6:21	122
12:7	96
16:19-31	124
22:3-4	24
22:54-62	147
23:42	125
23:43	125

John

2:3-4	162
6:38	163
7:6	163
13:1	163
10:10	24
10:27-29	8, 14
11:25	117
14:1-3	117, 120
19:28-30	164
20:25	117

Acts

2:44	33
9:4-5	97
9:11-12	97
9:13	97
9:15-16	98
9:17-19	98
13:13	147
13:22	119

Romans

8:31	12
8:37	166
8:38-39	14
9:20-21	138
12:1-2	57
12:17, 19	61

1Corinthians

2:9	64

2Corinthians

5:17	57
5:8	125
10:4-5	22
10:5	159

Hebrews

11:1	79
12:15	60
13:8	39

1John 4:8

4:8	63

Revelation

4:7	121
21:10	120
22:1	120
22:2	120